D1378966

100 GREAT
ITALIAN RECIPES

The Taunton Press

EDITED BY

ACADEMIA BARILLA

PHOTOGRAPHS

ALBERTO ROSSI

RECIPES BY

CHEF MARIO GRAZIA
CHEF LUCA ZANGA

TEXT BY

MARIAGRAZIA VILLA

ACADEMIA BARILLA EDITORIAL COORDINATION

CHATO MORANDI
ILARIA ROSSI
REBECCA PICKRELL

GRAPHIC DESIGN

MARIA CUCCHI

In the heart of Parma, one of the most illustrious capitals of Italian gastronomy, Academia Barilla was founded in 2004. The world's first international center dedicated to promoting Italian cuisine, protecting the legacy of regional gastronomy, and safeguarding against imitations and counterfeits, Academia Barilla is also a highly professional training center. It organizes cooking classes for cooking enthusiasts, provides resources for the food service industries, and offers products of the highest quality. In 2007, Academia Barilla received the "Premio Impresa Cultura" award, which honored its campaigns to promote the culture and creativity of Italian gastronomy throughout the world.

The Center was designed to meet the needs and training requirements of the food world, and is equipped with all of the multimedia services necessary for organizing major events: an auditorium with a viewing kitchen, a sensory analysis laboratory, and several classrooms equipped with the latest technology. The gastronomic library contains over 10,000 volumes and an impressive collection of historical menus, as well as art prints with culinary themes. The library's vast cultural heritage can be consulted on the Internet, and offers access to hundreds of digitally archived historical texts.

With its cutting-edge approach and its team of internationally renowned experts, Academia Barilla offers a vast range of courses that meet the needs of both restaurant chefs and amateur food lovers. In 2011, a rich offering of Food Tours was initiated, aimed at discovering the regions, products, and typical recipes of Italy. Further, under the supervision of experts, chefs, and food critics, Academia Barilla organizes cultural events and activities on the art of cooking, which are open to the public.

CONTENTS

INTRODUCTION

Italy has a vast array of culinary masterpieces. Such a broad palette of colors, which are different in every single geographic area, and within each geographic area, differing by individual territory, and in each individual city. It is truly the destination of the new Grand Tour, which now not only seeks beauty in archaeology, architecture, art, or landscapes, but also in time-honored delicacies with a modern heart. Here, history, climate, environment, manual dexterity, and culinary genius have merged, and continue to blend into an inimitable harmony.

Artichoke salad with Parmigiano-Reggiano cheese; Penne All'Arrabbiata; Branzino All'Acqua Pazza; mixed fish fry; capon stuffed with chestnuts; asparagus with Parmigiano-Reggiano cheese; Baci di Dama with cacao; peaches with amaretti; zabaglione. This is a mere glimpse of a possible gastronomic itinerary along the Italian peninsula, and the list goes on. It is estimated that in Italy there are over 3000 typical dishes, just counting the funda-

mental ones. There are many more, if we take into account the numerous creative variants that each recipe has carried along with itself over time. For this volume, the Academia Barilla has selected 100 easy recipes from Italian cuisine, all characterized by the same straightforward execution. While being quite aware of having left out many others, we have collected those considered the best—for quality, truth, and wisdom—for raising awareness of the primacy of Italian cuisine. In these recipes, respect for the territory—seen not only as a physical space, but also social and cultural—and investment into the legacy of the past have come together, with a pinch of poetry and innovation.

Not only the typical dishes have been consecrated by tradition, but also the creations that are typically Italian for their successful alchemy of gastronomic intuition, executive ability, and use of great products typical of the Bel Paese. Examples include buffalo mozzarella from Campania, Pecorino Ro-

THE ELEGANCE OF SIMPLICITY

mano, radicchio di Treviso, Taggiasca olives, balsamic vinegar of Modena, Sicilian pistachios, and Piedmontese hazelnuts. And in the culinary universe of the peninsula, even though there are dishes with considerable complexity, the overwhelming majority are characterized by the elegance of simplicity: They require just a few ingredients of very high quality, and the creativity and care to bring out their best in just a few steps. Perhaps this is because the majority of the jewels of Italian cuisine—which also include many recipes of aristocratic ancestry—come from dishes with a humble origin, and were born making use of inexpensive, everyday ingredients, yet filled with imagination and flavor. For example, classic Vermicelli with Tomato Sauce has exquisite originality because of its very simplicity. Such recipes have turned necessity into a virtue. These are simple preparations, but were quickly admitted into the most esteemed dining halls, and have now risen to the ranks of refined specialties.

Some of them can boast service for centuries, if not millennia. Just think of the traditional cream of fava beans. Even the ancient Romans had a passion for this legume, as proven by their many recipes still used on the peninsula today. Other dishes are more recent, yet have already entered into the Olympus of the most representative recipes of Italy. The gourmet Tiramisu, for example, one of the most well-known spoon desserts, was born in a restaurant in Treviso, in the Veneto region, in the late 1960s.

The fame of Italian cuisine, however, depends not only upon the delicacy of the dishes themselves, prepared with skill and with quality products, but also upon the way it expresses the significance of a good life. The food is a metaphor for a lifestyle that is typically Italian: sunny, open, creative, and joyful, where good humor gives you an appetite, and vice versa. And this philosophy—an outlook on the kitchen, but also on the world—is something that all Italians have in common.

APPETIZERS

WELL BEGUN...

Like a quotation at the beginning of the novel, the appetizer should take inspiration from the overall menu, allowing diners to speculate as to the meal's character and flavors. Its purpose is to whet the appetite, without satiating it and removing the taste for what will come later.

Within the structure of the Italian meal, the concept of the appetizer was born in the mid-19th century. From the so-called "service à la française," echoing gargantuan Renaissance and Baroque banquets, in which all the dishes were available to the diners, to later alternating "buffet services" (i.e., cold foods) with "kitchen services" (hot foods), the next step was toward the more rational and elegant "Russian style service," essentially still in use, where the various courses are served at the table one after the other in a specific order.

While Italian appetizers traditionally include a plate of cold cuts (every region in Italy has their own excellent versions) served with vegetables marinated in oil or vinegar, sometimes with curls of fresh butter or fruit (like the famous Parma ham accompanied by slices of melon, figs, or grapes), the gastronomic genius of the Bel Paese has many ways to start things off. Appetizers can be cold, like the Artichoke Salad with Parmigiano-Reggiano cheese; room temperature, like the Potato Salad with Chicken and Focaccia; or hot, like the Fried Squash Blossoms. They can be classified as "of the land" if they are meat-based, like the famous Veal with Tuna Sauce; "of the sea," if they focus on fish or seafood, like the Salad of Spelt and Shrimps; or as "from the garden," like those using primarily vegetables, such as the Broccoli Flan with Anchovy Sauce.

The opening of the meal may be simple, if it consists of one single course, or complex, if presented as a set of various dishes, and in Italy this is becoming a more fashionable way to enjoy the appetizers. That beginning of the meal becomes the star, in the form of small, numerous, and varied snacks, accompanied by a glass of good wine. When appetizers aren't limited to starting off the dinner, these tiny delicacies still fully satisfy, but with a certain lightness.

BROCCOLI FLAN
WITH ANCHOVY SAUCE

Difficulty: 1

Preparation: 30 minutes
Cooking: 40 minutes

4 SERVINGS

9 oz. (250 g) **broccoli**, or about 1 1/2 cups florets
2/3 cup (150 ml) **cream**
1 oz. (25 g) grated **Parmigiano-Reggiano cheese**, or about 1/4 cup
3 large **eggs**
2 tsp. (10 g) **unsalted butter**
salt and pepper

FOR THE SAUCE
2 **salted anchovies**
2 tbsp. (30 ml) **extra-virgin olive oil**

Heat the oven to 300°F (150°C). Boil a medium pot of salted water. Add the broccoli and cook until the stems are tender when pierced with a fork. Plunge in ice water, then drain.

Put the broccoli in a blender. Add the cream, Parmigiano-Reggiano cheese, and eggs. Blend until smooth. Season with salt and pepper.

Butter individual ramekins or timbale molds and fill with the broccoli mixture. Put the ramekins in a hot water bath (a bain-marie or a roasting pan filled with hot water halfway up the sides of the ramekins) and bake for about 40 minutes.

Meanwhile, prepare the anchovy sauce. Rinse the anchovies, fillet them if necessary, put them in the blender with the oil and blend until smooth.

When the flans are cooked, remove them from the water bath and let them cool slightly. Invert the flans onto individual serving plates and garnish with the anchovy sauce.

9 oz. (250 g) **buffalo mozzarella**
3 1/2 tbsp. (52 ml) **extra-virgin olive oil**; more for drizzling
4 **ripe tomatoes**
1/2 oz. (15 g) **fresh basil**, or about 30 leaves
sugar
garlic, finely sliced
fresh thyme
salt and pepper

Difficulty: 1

Preparation: 10 minutes
Cooking: 50 minutes

BUFFALO MOZZARELLA AND SEMI-CANDIED TOMATOES

Heat the oven to 200°F (100°C). Slice the tomatoes, and arrange them on a baking sheet. Sprinkle with salt, a little sugar, the garlic, and thyme. Drizzle with olive oil and bake for about an hour.

Meanwhile, bring a medium pot of water to a boil. Dip the basil in the water and then plunge into ice water. Puree the basil leaves in a blender with the 3 1/2 tbsp. (50 ml) olive oil. Slice the mozzarella and season lightly with salt and pepper. Make the stacks by layering the mozzarella and semi-candied tomato slices. Drizzle with olive oil and garnish with the basil sauce.

1/4 lb. (120 g) **puff pastry**,
  or 1 sheet
1 3/4 oz. (50 g) **pancetta**
  or thick bacon, diced
1/2 lb. (250 g) **potatoes**
1/2 cup (125 ml) **milk**
1 large **egg**
1 sprig **fresh rosemary**,
  leaves chopped
salt and pepper

Difficulty: 1

Preparation: 1 hour
Cooking: 15 minutes

POTATO AND BACON TARTLETS

Boil the potatoes, skin on, in a saucepan of lightly salted water until tender but firm, 15 minutes.

Drain, cool, and peel them, and dice or slice into rounds.

Heat the oven to 350°F (180°C).

On a clean work surface, roll out the puff pastry to a thickness of 2 mm (1/12 in). Cut into four equal pieces. Line four individual tartlet molds with the puff pastry, and fill the molds with the pancetta and potatoes. Put the molds on a baking sheet.

In a bowl, whisk the egg together with the milk, salt and pepper, and the rosemary. Pour the mixture into the tartlet molds and bake for about 15 minutes.

FLATBREADS WITH CREAMY OREGANO-FLAVORED RICOTTA AND OLIVE PESTO

Difficulty: 2

Preparation: 30 minutes
Resting: 30 minutes
Cooking: 12 minutes

4 SERVINGS

FOR THE DOUGH
1 3/4 cups plus 1 1/2 tbsp. (250 g) **Italian "00" flour**
1/4 cup plus 1 1/2 tbsp. (80 ml) **extra-virgin olive oil**
1/2 cup (120 ml) **water**
3/4 tsp. (5 g) **salt**

FOR THE FILLING
0.35 lbs. (160 g) **fresh ricotta**
0.5 oz. (15 g) **fresh oregano**, or about 2 tbsp. + 2 tsp.
2.8 oz. (80 g) **black olive pesto**, or about 3/4 cup
1 tbsp. plus 2 tsp. (25 ml) **extra-virgin olive oil**
salt and pepper

FOR THE GARNISH
Mixed greens, as needed
2 tbsp. (30 ml) **extra-virgin olive oil**

Mix the flour with the oil, water and a pinch of salt until a smooth and homogenous dough forms. Wrap it in plastic and refrigerate for 30 minutes.
Heat the oven to 350°F (180°C). On a clean work surface, use a rolling pin or pasta machine to roll out sheets of dough about 1/16 inch (2 mm) thick. Using a fluted pastry wheel, cut out 3-inch (8 cm) dough squares. Transfer the squares to a baking sheet lined with parchment and bake for about 12 minutes.
Whisk the ricotta with the oil, oregano, olive pesto, salt and pepper. Spoon the mixture into a pastry bag and pipe a bit of filling onto a square of dough. Place another square on top, like a sandwich. Repeat with the remaining squares and filling. Garnish with mixed greens and drizzle with the olive oil.

FOR THE MEAT

1 1/3 lbs. (600 g) **boned veal eye round**
1/4 cup 6 3/4 tbsp. (100 ml) **extra-virgin olive oil**
1 clove **garlic**
rosemary and sage to taste
salt

FOR THE SAUCE

1/2 cup (100 ml) **white wine**
2 **anchovies in salt**, rinsed and dried
1 oz. (30 g) **day-old bread**
10 tsp. (50 ml) **wine vinegar**
5 **capers in salt**, rinsed
8 3/4 oz. (250 g) **tuna in oil**
3 large hard-cooked **eggs**
Veal or beef stock as needed

Difficulty: 2

Preparation: 40 minutes
Cooking: 40 minutes

CHILLED VEAL IN TUNA SAUCE

Heat the oven to 350°F (180°C). Salt the veal and brown it in oil in a Dutch oven or heavy-duty roasting pan over medium heat, about 4 minutes per side. Add the garlic and the herbs, and roast until medium-rare (an instant read thermometer inserted in the center of the meat should read 140°), about 1 hour. Remove the meat from the pan and transfer to a cutting board to rest. Put the stale bread and the vinegar in a bowl. Let the bread soak, and then squeeze it dry and discard the vinegar. Deglaze the roasting pan with white wine, and simmer until the wine evaporates. Add the capers, anchovies, tuna and bread, and cook for a few minutes.
Transfer the sauce mixture to a blender. Add the yolks from the hard-boiled eggs and blend, gradually adding the beef or veal stock until the sauce is smooth and creamy. Thinly slice the veal and serve with the sauce.

12 **vol-au-vents** (puff
pastry shells)
6 oz. (170 g) **Fontina
cheese**, coarsely
chopped
1 1/4 cups (300 ml)
lukewarm milk
2 large **egg yolks**
2 tsp. (5 g) **all-purpose
flour**
black truffle (optional)
10 1/2 oz. (300 g)
radicchio, finely
chopped
salt

VOL-AU-VENT WITH RADICCHIO AND FONDUE

In a bowl, whisk the egg yolks with 2 tbsp. milk. In another bowl, blend the flour into the remaining milk and add the Fontina. Transfer to a saucepan and cook over medium heat, whisking vigorously with a metal whisk, until the mixture thickens.
Add the egg yolks mixture, reduce the heat to low, and continue to cook, whisking occasionally, for about 10 minutes. Remove from the heat. Add the radicchio to the cheese mixture and season with salt. Evenly distribute the cheese mixture among the the vol-au-vents and serve, garnished with the black truffle, if using.

Difficulty: 1

Preparation: 10 minutes
Cooking: 15 minutes

12 **zucchini flowers**
olive oil for frying, as needed
salt
flour, as needed

FOR THE BATTER
1 cup (200 ml) **cold water**
1 1/2 cups (200 g) **pastry flour**
1 large **egg**

Difficulty: 2

Preparation: 20 minutes

Cooking: 5-6 minutes

FRIED ZUCCHINI FLOWERS

Prepare the zucchini flowers by removing the pistils, taking care not to tear the delicate flowers.
In a bowl, whisk together the batter ingredients.
Heat the oil in a skillet over medium heat until very hot. Flour the flowers lightly, dip them in the batter, and and fry them in batches until golden, transferring them to a paper towel lined rack to drain. Sprinkle with salt, transfer to a serving plate and serve hot.

4 **artichokes**
1 cup plus 3 tbsp. (120 g)
  **Parmigiano-Reggiano
  cheese**, grated or
  shaved
Juice of 2 **lemons**, plus
  zest for garnish, if
  desired
4-5 **fresh mint leaves**,
  torn
3 1/2 tbsp. (50 ml) **extra-
  virgin olive oil**,
  preferably Ligurian;
  more for drizzling
salt and pepper

Difficulty: 1

Preparation: 20 minutes

ARTICHOKE SALAD
WITH PARMIGIANO-REGGIANO

Trim the artichokes, removing the outer leaves and spines. Trim the stems and soak them in a mixture of water and lemon juice for 15 minutes.

In a bowl, whisk together the lemon juice, olive oil and a pinch of salt and pepper. Cut the artichokes in half, removing any tough inner fibers. Scoop out the fuzzy choke with a melon ball cutter.

Just before serving, slice the artichokes very thinly (you can use a Japanese mandolin or other adjustable blade slicer). Transfer to a bowl, and dress them with the lemon juice and olive oil mixture. Arrange the artichokes in the center of four serving plates. Top each salad with the Parmigiano-Reggiano, mint, and a drizzle of olive oil. Garnish with the lemon zest, if using.

3/4 cup (150 g) **spelt**

12 **shrimp**

3 1/2 oz. (100 g) **carrots**, cut into small dice

3 1/2 oz. (100 g) **zucchini**, cut into small dice

3 1/2 oz. (100 g) **tomato**, peeled, seeded, and diced

1 3/4 oz. (50 g) **peas**, or about 1/3 cup

1 3/4 oz. (50 g) **red onion**, finely chopped

1 tsp. **minced fresh parsley**

6 **fresh basil leaves**, torn

3 1/2 tbsp. (50 ml) **extra-virgin olive oil**

salt and pepper

Difficulty: 1

Preparation: 30 minutes

Cooking: 10 minutes

WARM SPELT SALAD WITH SHRIMP

Bring a small saucepan of salted water to a boil. Add the peas and cook them until just tender. Drain and rinse the peas under cold water.

Heat 1 tbsp. plus 2 tsp. of the oil in a skillet over medium heat. Add the onion and cook, stirring, until tender. Add the zucchini and carrots and season with salt and pepper. Cook until lightly browned but not softened. Add the blanched peas. Remove from the heat.

Boil the spelt in salted water, strain it and put it in a bowl. Add the cooked vegetables, tomato, parsley, and hand-torn basil. Drizzle with olive oil and salt to taste. Sauté the shrimp in a bit of oil and serve them with the spelt salad.

3 **green apples**, 2 diced
and 1 thinly sliced for
garnish
7 oz. (200 g) **radicchio**,
thinly sliced
10 1/2 oz. (300 g) **chicken
breast**
3 1/2 oz. (100 g) **focaccia**,
cut into cubes
1/4 cup (20 g) **sliced
almonds**
1/3 cup plus 1 1/2 tbsp.
(100 ml) **extra-virgin
olive oil**
1 tbsp. plus 1 tsp.(20 ml)
vinegar
salt and pepper

Difficulty: 1

Preparation: 30 minutes
Cooking: 20 minutes

APPLE, CHICKEN
AND TOASTED FOCACCIA SALAD

Heat the oven 350°F (180°C). Season the chicken with salt and pepper, then drizzle with olive oil. Bake for 18 to 20 minutes (alternatively, you can grill it). Let cool, then cut into cubes.
Spread the focaccia on a baking sheet and toast in the oven for 5 minutes.
Put the radicchio in a bowl. Dress with the olive oil and vinegar and season with salt and pepper. Add the apples, chicken, focaccia and almonds. Distribute the salad among individual bowls and garnish with the sliced apples.

FIRST COURSES

A RECORD FOR TASTE

A gastronomic galaxy in terms of shapes, colors, fragrances, styles, and flavors, the primo, the first course dish in Italian cuisine, is a practically unlimited world of combinations and variations. In recent years it has taken on an even greater importance within the meal, both at home and in restaurants. It is not called primo (the first course dish) for reasons of hierarchy, but rather for temporal reasons, because it is served before the secondo (the second, or main course dish), but it still is the "Prince" among courses. It is also leaning more and more toward becoming a single-course meal, capable of providing both carbohydrates and proteins. Even the simplest of recipes, like Bucatini Cacio e Pepe, can act as a clear example.

The most popular primo in Italy is undoubtedly pasta, and it is prepared in thousands of different ways. It can be fresh and kneaded with eggs, traditionally prepared with meat sauce, and usually intended for holidays and important banquets, like Tagliatelle with Bolognese Sauce. Or it can be dried, used for more everyday consumption, and found in over a hundred shapes, both long—like linguine, ziti, or spaghetti—and short—like penne, fusilli, or farfalle. It can be served drained and tossed with a sauce, or it can be served in broth, like the delicious Passatelli from Emilia.

Rice also figures among the most highly-prized first course dishes in the Italian meal. Arriving from the Orient in the 15th century, it found a country of choice in Italy, which today produces the best quality rice in the world. A discreet and delicate foodstuff, it can welcome any sort of sauce, and it can give rise to recipes that are completely straightforward, as well as complex and sensational recipes for risottos and timbales.

For millennia, soups and broths have occupied a place on the Italian table. There is a wide selection of them in the cuisine of the peninsula, and many use vegetables, perhaps because of the high esteem in which the Mediterranean tradition has always held fresh produce. These are simple dishes of peasant origin—from Pasta e Fagioli to Minestrone Soup—and connected with slower rhythms of life and a closer relationship with the seasons and nature, but still able to satisfy our desire for appetizing food.

SEAFOOD PASTA

Preparation: 40 minutes
Cooking: 8 minutes

4 Servings

10 2/3 oz. (300 g) **bavette** or other thin ribbon-shaped pasta
14 oz. (400 g) **mussels**, scrubbed and debearded
14 oz. (400 g) **clams**, scrubbed and rinsed
4 small **red mullet**, gutted, filleted, and washed
4 **shrimp**, peeled (leave tail segment intact) and deveined

5 oz. (150g) **cherry tomatoes**, cut into quarters
1 cup (150 ml) **white wine**
1 clove **garlic**
1 tbsp. **fresh parsley**, chopped
1 bunch **fresh basil**
1 sprig **fresh oregano**
1/3 cup (80 ml) **extra-virgin olive oil**
salt and pepper

Bring a pot of well-salted water to a boil. Cook the bavette until al dente, and drain. While the pasta cooks, roughly chop the oregano leaves and tear the basil by hand. Heat the oil in a skillet with the garlic and parsley, and add the oregano and basil. Add the mussels, clams, and white wine. Cover with a lid and cook, removing the shellfish as they open and discarding any that don't open. Remove them from the saucepan, shell three-quarters of them, and transfer them to a bowl.

To the same skillet, add the red mullet, all of the shrimp, and the tomatoes. Cook, stirring, for a few minutes; the sauce should still be fairly liquid. Add the mussels and the clams. Season with salt and pepper to taste. Transfer the cooked pasta to the skillet with the sauce, cook briefly to meld the flavors, and serve.

10 oz. (300 g) **bavette** or other thin ribbon-shaped pasta

10 oz. (300 g) **swordfish**, cut into cubes

10 oz. (300 g) **cherry tomatoes**, cut in half

3 tbsp. (40 ml) **extra-virgin olive oil**

1 clove **garlic**

wild fennel or sprig of fresh dill

chile pepper, chopped

salt and pepper

Difficulty: 1

Preparation: 20 minutes

Cooking: 10 minutes

NOODLES WITH SWORDFISH, CHERRY TOMATOES AND WILD FENNEL

Bring a pot of well-salted water to a boil.

In a nonstick skillet over medium-high heat, heat a little of the olive oil until hot. Add the swordfish and sear. Season with salt, pepper, and the sprig of wild fennel or dill, previously washed and dried.

Pour the rest of the oil into another skillet. Add the garlic clove and the chile and cook until the garlic is lightly browned. Sprinkle half of the tomatoes with salt, add them to the skillet, and cook cook for another couple of minutes. Add the fish.

While the sauce cooks, cook the pasta in salted boiling water until al dente. Drain and add directly to the pan with the sauce. Cook for a few seconds, and serve.

12 oz. (350 g) **bucatini**
6 oz. (150 g) **guanciale** or
   pancetta
14 oz. (400 g) **ripe
   tomatoes**
1 **dried red chile**,
   crumbled
scant 1/2 cup (40 g)
   grated or shaved
   Pecorino Romano
salt and pepper

Difficulty: 1

Preparation: 15 minutes
Cooking: 8-10 minutes

BUCATINI ALLA AMATRICIANA

Bring a pot of well-salted water to a boil.

Cut the guanciale or pancetta into slices, and then into rectangles. Put in a skillet over low heat,

add a very small amount of water, and simmer to render the fat.

Meanwhile, peel and seed the tomatoes and dice them. Remove the guanciale or pancetta from the pan and drain thoroughly. Add the tomatoes to the fat in the pan. Season with the crumbled chile pepper and salt and pepper. Return the guanciale or pancetta to the sauce in the pan and heat briefly.

Meanwhile, cook the bucatini in the boiling water until al dente. Drain, combine well with the sauce, and serve.

12 oz. (350 g) **bucatini**
6 3/4 tbsp. (100 ml) **extra-virgin olive oil**
7 oz. (200 g) **Pecorino Romano cheese**, grated
Coarsely ground **black pepper**

Difficulty: 1

Preparation: 10 minutes
Cooking: 6 minutes

BUCATINI WITH CHEESE AND PEPPER

Bring a pot of well-salted water to a boil. Cook the bucatini in the boiling water until al dente. Drain the pasta, return to the pot, and add the oil, Pecorino, and black pepper to taste; the amount can range from a light sprinkling to a generous handful. Serve immediately.

10 1/2 oz. (300 g) **farfalle** (bowties) or fusilli
1 1/2 lb. (700 g) **eggplant**
2 tbsp. (30 ml) **extra-virgin olive oil**
oil for frying (optional)
1 bunch **basil**
salt and pepper

FARFALLE WITH WHITE EGGPLANT SAUCE

Bring a saucepan of well-salted water to a boil. Cut the eggplant flesh into large pieces.
Boil in the salted water until softened, about 10 minutes. Drain and transfer the eggplant to a blender. Add the basil leaves and a pinch of salt and pepper. Blend until you have a smooth, thick sauce. Season to taste with salt and pepper and keep warm over medium heat.
Bring a large pot of well salted water to a boil. Cook the pasta until al dente, drain, and add to the sauce. Add the extra-virgin olive oil and cook briefly, stirring. Transfer to pasta dishes and serve. (If you like, try garnishing with thinly sliced eggplant skin briefly fried in oil.)

Difficulty: 1

Preparation: 15 minutes
Cooking: 12 minutes

FUSILLI PASTA SALAD WITH VEGETABLES AND SQUID

Difficulty: 1

Preparation: 15 minutes
Cooking: 10 minutes

4 Servings

14 oz. (400 g) **fusilli**
3 1/2 oz. (100 g) **carrots** or about 2 small, peeled
12 1/2 oz. (360 g) **zucchini**, or about 3 small
10 1/2 oz. (300 g) **artichokes**
10 1/2 oz. (300 g) **squid**
Leafy herbs, as needed
1/4 cup (60 ml) **extra-virgin olive oil**
juice of 1 **lemon**
salt and white pepper
3 1/2 oz. (100 g) **Swiss chard**, sliced

Remove the tough outer leaves from the artichokes. Cut each artichokes in half lengthwise and scoop out the fuzzy choke with a melon ball cutter. In a bowl, combine water and some of the lemon juice. Cut the artichokes into narrow strips and let soak in the lemon juice mixture to prevent them from browning.
Cut the carrots and zucchini into thin, narrow strips.
Clean the squid by removing the skin from the body and cutting the tentacles from the body. Flip back the tentacles and squeeze out and discard the beak located in the center of the tentacles. Remove the eyes, the entrails, and the transparent inner cartilage. Then cut the body into very thin strips.
Bring a pot of well-salted water to a boil. Add the pasta, and 5 minutes before it is cooked, add the vegetables to the water. Stir and cook for 3 minutes, then add the squid for the last 2 minutes. Drain, add a little oil, and transfer everything to a tray and to cool. When cool, dress with the rest of the oil and lemon juice, and season with salt and white pepper. Serve on a bed of fresh aromatic herbs and Swiss chard.

10 1/2 oz. lb (300 g) **fusilli** or sedani rigati

2 tbsp. (30 ml) **extra-virgin olive oil**

9 oz. (250 g) **radicchio**, cut into strips

4 oz. (120 g) **speck**, cut into strips

2/3 cup (150 ml) **heavy cream**

1 1/2 oz. (40 g) **shallots, sliced**

salt and pepper

Difficulty: 2

Preparation: 20 minutes
Cooking: 12 minutes

FUSILLI WITH SPECK AND RADICCHIO

Bring a pot of well-salted pot water to a boil.

In a skillet, heat the oil over low heat until hot. Add the shallots and cook, stirring, until browned, 3 to 4 minutes. Raise the heat to medium, add the speck, and cook, stirring, for another 2 to 3 minutes to soften. Add the cream, season with salt and pepper, and lower the heat to low. Simmer until slightly reduced.

Meanwhile, cook the pasta in the boiling water until al dente and drain. Combine the pasta thoroughly with the sauce and serve.

10.5 oz. (300 g) **penne lisce** or farfalle
1 1/2 lb. (650 g) **butternut squash**, peeled and cut into small dice
7 oz. (200 g) **pancetta**, thinly sliced
2 oz. (50 g) **yellow onion**, chopped
1 3/4 tbsp. (25 g) **unsalted butter**
fresh thyme
salt and pepper

Difficulty: 1

Preparation: 30 minutes
Cooking: 8 minutes

PENNE LISCE WITH SQUASH AND PANCETTA

Heat the oven to 300°F (150°C). Spread the pancetta on a baking sheet and bake until crunchy, about 15 minutes.

Put half of the squash, the onion, and a pinch of salt in a saucepan. Fill with enough water to cover, bring to a boil, and cook until the squash is tender. Drain, transfer to a blender, and puree until smooth.

Melt the butter in a skillet over medium heat. Add the thyme and cook, stirring, until fragrant. Add the remaining squash, season with salt and pepper, and continue to cook until tender. Add the pureed squash mixture and heat through.

Bring a pot of well-salted water to a boil. Cook the pasta in the boiling water until al dente. Drain the pasta, add it to the sauce, and cook briefly to combine. Transfer the pasta to pasta dishes, garnish with the pancetta, and serve.

SICILIAN EGGPLANT RIGATONI

Difficulty: 1

Preparation: 1 hour
Cooking: 10 minutes

4 Servings

12 oz. (350 g) **rigatoni**
9 oz. (250 g) **eggplant**
2 tbsp. (30 ml) **extra-virgin olive oil**
2 oz. (50 g) **yellow onion**, roughly chopped
1 clove **garlic**
2 lbs. (1 kg) **ripe tomatoes**, diced
6 leaves fresh **basil**
2 oz. (50 g) **grated ricotta salata**, or about 1/2 cup
salt and pepper
flour as needed
extra-virgin olive oil, as needed for frying

Dice or cut the eggplant into sticks, then put it in a colander, salt it lightly and allow it to drain for about 30 minutes.
In a skillet, heat the oil over medium-high heat until hot. Toss the eggplant with flour and fry until golden. Transfer to a paper towel-lined plate.
Add the onion to the skillet along with garlic clove. Add tomatoes, season with salt and pepper, and cook for about 10 minutes; then pass the mixture through a food mill. Add the eggplant to the tomato sauce.
Bring a pot of well-salted water to a boil. Cook the rigatoni until al dente, drain, and pour it into a large bowl. Add the sauce, stir, and then add the basil. Transfer to bowls, sprinkle with the ricotta salata, and serve.

10.5 oz. (300 g) **penne rigate** or tortiglioni
1 1/2 lb. (600 g) **peeled, diced tomatoes**
2 tbsp. (30 ml) **extra-virgin olive oil**
0.7 oz. (20 g) **fresh parsley**, chopped
2 cloves **garlic**, sliced
1 **red chile**, fresh or dried
salt

Difficulty: 1

Preparation: 30 minutes
Cooking: 11 minutes

PENNE RIGATE ALL'ARRABBIATA

Bring a pot of well-salted water to a boil.
Using kitchen gloves, slice the chili, if fresh, or crumble it, if dried. In a large skillet, heat the oil until hot. Add the garlic and chile and cook until browned, taking care that they don't darken too much. Add the tomatoes, season with salt, and cook over a high heat for about 15 minutes, stirring occasionally.
Cook the pasta in the boiling water until al dente. Drain, combine with the sauce, and serve garnished with the parsley.

12 oz. (350 g) **spaghetti**
5 oz. (150 g) **guanciale** or bacon
4 large **egg yolks**
3 1/2 oz. (100 g) **Pecorino Romano**
salt and pepper

SPAGHETTI ALLA CARBONARA

Difficulty: 1

Preparation: 10 minutes
Cooking: 8 minutes

In a bowl, beat the egg yolks with a pinch of salt and a little of the Pecorino cheese.
Bring a pot of well-salted water to a boil.
Cut the bacon into slices about 1/12 inch thick (2mm) and then into strips, or dice them. In a skillet, cook the bacon until lightly browned.
Cook the spaghetti in the boiling water until al dente. Drain the pasta, reserving some of the cooking water. Transfer the pasta to the skillet with the bacon and cook briefly, stirring. Remove from the heat and add the beaten egg yolks and a little of the cooking water, and stir for about 30 seconds.
Add the remaining Pecorino, stir again, and serve immediately.

SPAGHETTI WITH CLAMS

Difficulty: 1

Preparation: 20 minutes
Cooking: 8 minutes

4 SERVINGS

12 oz. (350 g) **spaghetti**
2 1/4 lbs. (1 kg) **clams**, scrubbed
6 3/4 tbsp. (100 ml) **extra-virgin olive oil**
1 tbsp. chopped fresh **parsley**
1 clove **garlic,** chopped
salt and pepper

Bring a pot of well-salted water to a boil.

Heat 1 tbsp. of the oil in a large skillet. Add the clams, cover, and cook until they open, 2-3 minutes. Remove the skillet from the heat. Remove some of the clams from their shells, strain the cooking liquid, and then pour it back into the skillet with the clams. Set aside.

In another skillet, heat the remaining oil until hot. Add the garlic and cook until browned. Add the clams and their liquid and bring to a boil.

Meanwhile, cook the spaghetti in the boiling water until al dente. Drain, reserving some of the pasta water. Add the pasta to the clam mixture, adding a little pasta water if you want a wetter dish. Transfer to pasta bowls and serve, sprinkled generously with the pepper and the parsley.

TAGLIATELLE BOLOGNESE

Difficulty: 2

Preparation: 1 hour
30 minutes

Cooking: 3-4 minutes

4 Servings

FOR THE TAGLIATELLE
2 cups plus 3 tbsp. (300 g) **pastry flour**
3 large **eggs**

FOR THE SAUCE
2/3 cup (160 ml) **water**
5 1/3 oz. (150 g) **ground pork**
5 1/3 oz. (150 g) **ground beef**
5 oz. (150 g) **lard**
1 1/2 oz. (40 g) **carrots**, chopped

1 1/2 oz. (40 g) **celery**, chopped
1 1/2 oz. (40 g) **yellow onions**, chopped
3 oz. (90 g) **tomato paste**
1/2 cup (100 ml) **red wine**
1/4 cup plus 2 3/4 tbsp. (100 ml) **extra-virgin olive oil**
2 **bay leaves**
1 1/2 oz. (40 g) grated **Parmigiano-Reggiano cheese**, or about 1/2 cup
salt and pepper

To make the pasta, combine the flour with the eggs and knead until you have a smooth, homogeneous dough. Wrap the dough in plastic wrap and refrigerate for about 30 minutes.

Remove the dough from the refrigerator and, using a rolling pin or machine, roll it out into sheets about 1/25 inch (1mm) thick. Cut the sheets into strips about 1/4 inch (6-7mm) wide. Spread the tagliatelle out on a lightly floured work surface.

To make the sauce, break up the bay leaves very finely. In a pot or Dutch oven, sauté the lard, the chopped vegetables, and the bay leaves with the olive oil. When the vegetables are golden brown, add the meat and sauté on high heat. Add the red wine and cook until the liquid evaporates completely. Then lower the heat and stir in the tomato paste. Season with salt and freshly ground black pepper continue to cook on low heat for about an hour, adding a few spoonsful of water, if necessary.

Meanwhile, bring a pot of well-salted water to a boil. Cook the tagliatelle in the boiling water until al dente. Drain and pour the pasta a large bowl. Add the meat sauce, sprinkle with the Parmigiano-Reggiano, stir well, and serve.

TROFIE AL PESTO

Difficulty: 2

Preparation: 30 minutes

Resting: 30 minutes

Cooking: 5 minutes

FOR THE PASTA
2 1/2 cups (300 g) **"o" type flour**
2/3 cup (150 ml) **water**
or: 14 oz. (400 g) **ready-made pasta**

FOR THE SAUCE
1 oz. (30 g) **fresh basil**
1/2 oz. (15 g) **pine nuts**, or about 2 tbsp.
2 oz. (60 g) **Parmigiano-Reggiano**

1 oz. (40 g) **grated Pecorino**, or about 1/2 cup
1 clove **garlic**
3 1/2 oz. (100 g) **green beans**, cut into thirds
7 oz. (200 g) **potatoes**, diced
3/4 cup plus 1 1/2 tbsp. (200 ml) **extra-virgin olive oil** (preferably from Liguria); more as needed
salt

To make the pasta, mound the flour on a work surface. Make a well in the center and knead with sufficient water to make firm elastic dough. Cover the dough with plastic wrap and let rest for 30 minutes before using.

When the dough is ready, break off small pieces the size of chickpeas, and roll them in your hands (or roll them on the work surface, pressing down lightly at the same time) to make the trofie. Or, cook the pasta.

To make the sauce, wash and dry the basil. Using a mortar and pestle, crush the basil, pine nuts and garlic with 1/2 cup plus 2 tbsp. (150 ml) of the olive oil, a pinch of salt, and the cheese. (Alternatively, pulse the ingredients in a food processor.) When the ingredients are well mixed, transfer the mixture to a bowl and cover with the remaining olive oil.

Boil the potatoes and the green beans separately. When the vegetables are almost cooked, add the trofie to the same pan. Remove from the heat and drain, reserving some of the cooking water. Add the pesto and stir well, diluting with a little cooking water and a little extra-virgin olive oil.

4 Servings

10 1/2 oz. (300 g) **vermicelli** or spaghetti
1 1/2 lb. (600 g) **tomatoes**, peeled and diced
3.5 oz. (100 g) **yellow onion**, chopped
2 tbsp. (30 ml) **extra-virgin olive oil**
8 leaves **fresh basil**, coarsely chopped
1 clove **garlic**
salt and pepper

Difficulty: 1

Preparation: 30 minutes
Cooking: 13 minutes

VERMICELLI WITH TOMATO SAUCE

Heat the oil in a skillet until hot. Add the onion and garlic and cook until golden brown. Add the tomatoes, season with salt and pepper, and continue to cook over a high heat for about 20 minutes, stirring occasionally. Remove the garlic and stir in the basil.
Bring a pot of well-salted water to a boil. Cook the pasta in the boiling water until al dente and drain. Transfer to bowls, pour the sauce over the pasta, and serve.

10 1/2 oz. (300 g) **vermicelli** or bucatini
5 oz. (150 g) **bacon** or guanciale, cut in small pieces
3 1/2 tbsp. (50 ml) **extra-virgin olive oil**
1 1/2 oz. (40 g) **Pecorino Romano**, grated, or about 1/2 cup
1 **red chile**, chopped
salt and pepper

Difficulty: 1

Preparation: 10 minutes
Cooking: 13 minutes

VERMICELLI ALLA GRICIA

Bring a pot of well-salted water to a boil.

In a skillet over medium heat, cook the bacon or guanciale for 3 minutes. Add the chile to taste.

Meanwhile, cook the pasta in the boiling water until al dente. Drain the pasta and add to the sauce.

Add the grated cheese and freshly ground black pepper to taste, and serve.

TOMATO RISOTTO

Difficulty: 1

Preparation: 30 minutes
Cooking: 16-18 minutes

4 SERVINGS

1 lb. (500 g) **ripe tomatoes**
1 tbsp. (15 ml) **extra-virgin olive oil**
10 oz. (300 g) **Vialone nano rice**, or about 1 1/2 cups
2 1/2 oz. (75 g) **small yellow onion**, chopped
scant 1/2 cup (100 ml) **dry white wine**
6 1/3 cups (1.5 liters) **vegetable hot stock**
1/4 cup (60 g) **butter**
3/4 cup (80 g) grated **Parmigiano-Reggiano cheese**
salt

Peel the and seed the tomatoes. Dice half of them and reserve.
In a small skillet, heat 1 tsp. of the oil. Add a third of the onion and cook until golden. Add the remaining tomatoes, season with salt, and cook over high heat for 10 minutes. Transfer to a blender, purée, and keep warm.
Meanwhile melt 4 tsp. of the butter in another pan. Add the remaining onion and cook until softened. Stir in the rice. Pour in the wine and simmer gently, stirring constantly, until the wine has evaporated completely. Continue to cook, adding half of the puréed tomato mixture and pouring in the stock a little at a time, stirring constantly. After about 10 minutes, add the reserved diced tomatoes.
When the rice-tomato mixture is cooked, season to taste. Remove from the heat and stir in the rest of the butter and the Parmigiano-Reggiano cheese.
Garnish with the remaining of the sauce.

1 1/4 (320 g) **Superfino or arborio rice**
2 3/4 oz. (80 g) **unsalted butter**
1 3/4 oz. (50 g) **yellow onion**
1/2 cup (100 ml) **white wine**
4 1/4 cups (1 l) **hot veal or beef stock**
Pinch of **saffron threads**
2 oz. (60 g) grated **Parmigiano-Reggiano cheese**, or about 2/3 cup
salt and pepper

Difficulty: 1

Preparation: 30 minutes
Cooking: 20 minutes

MILANESE-STYLE RISOTTO

In a saucepan or Dutch oven, melt half of the butter over medium heat. Add the onion and cook until softened. Stir in the rice and cook gently for 1 minute. Pour in the white wine, allow it to evaporate. Add the stock in increments and continue to cook. Five minutes before the rice has finished cooking, add the saffron and season with salt and pepper.
When all the liquid has been absorbed by the rice, but when it is still al dente, remove from the heat. Whisk in the remaining butter and Parmigiano-Reggiano.

11 1/2 oz. (320 g) **Arborio rice**
1/4 cup (60 ml) **extra-virgin olive oil**
8-10 **small crabs**, cut into quarters
5 cups (1.2 l) **hot fish stock**
3 1/2 tbsp. (50 ml) **white wine**
3 1/2 oz. (100 g) **squash blossoms**, cleaned and rinsed
1 1/2 tbsp. (10 g) grated **Pecorino Romano**
2 1/2 tbsp. (15 g) grated **Parmigiano-Reggiano**
1/3 cup plus 1 1/2 tbsp. (100 ml) **extra-virgin olive oil**
1 tbsp. **pine nuts**
1/4 clove **garlic**
1 tbsp. minced **fresh parsley**
salt and pepper

Difficulty: 1

Preparation: 10 minutes
Cooking: 20 minutes

SQUASH BLOSSOM RISOTTO WITH SMALL CRABS

Put the squash blossoms, pine nuts, grated Pecorino and Parmigiano, garlic, and oil in a blender, and puree. Season with salt and pepper to taste.

In a saucepan, heat the the oil until hot. Add the rice and toast it for a few minutes, stirring continuously. Add the white wine and cook until it has evaporated completely. Add the crabs and let them cook. Pour in lightly salted hot broth in increments. When all the liquid has been absorbed by the rice, but when it is still al dente and the crabs are cooked, remove from the heat. Stir in the extra-virgin olive oil and the squash blossom pesto, and serve sprinkled with the minced parsley.

RISOTTO WITH PORCINI MUSHROOMS

Difficulty: 1

Preparation: 20 minutes
Cooking: 18 minutes

4 Servings

1 1/2 cups (300 g) **Carnaroli rice**
2 1/2 oz. (75 g) **small onion**, chopped
6 1/3 cups (1.5 l) **hot veal or beef stock**
1/2 stick (57 g) **unsalted butter**
3/4 cup plus 1 tbsp. (80 g) **Parmigiano-Reggiano cheese**
4 tsp. (20 ml) **extra-virgin olive oil**
11 oz. (300 g) **porcini mushrooms**
1 clove **garlic**
1 tbsp. chopped **fresh parsley**
salt to taste

Clean the mushrooms thoroughly, removing the soil and wiping them with a damp cloth. Slice them thinly (reserve a few slices for garnish, if you like). In a skillet, heat the oil until hot. Add the garlic clove, cook until browned, and remove from the skillet. Add the mushrooms and cook, stirring, until tender but still firm. Lightly season with salt and stir in a little of the parsley. Melt 4 tbsp. of the butter in a saucepan. Add the onion and cook, stirring. Add the rice and toast it, stirring well to make sure it is coated with the butter. Continue to cook, adding the broth gradually and stirring often. About halfway through cooking, add the mushrooms. When the risotto is cooked, remove it from the heat and stir in the remaining butter and grated Parmigiano-Reggiano cheese. Garnish with the raw mushrooms, if using, and serve.

RISOTTO WITH SHRIMPS
AND ZUCCHINI FLOWERS

Difficulty: 1

Preparation: 20 minutes

Cooking: 20 minutes

4 Servings

10 1/2 oz. (300 g) **Arborio rice**
16 **zucchini flowers**
14 oz. (400 g) **shrimp**
6 1/3 cups (1.5 l) **hot fish stock**
1/2 **yellow onion**, finely chopped
extra-virgin olive oil, as needed
1 oz. (20 g) **unsalted butter**
salt
3 1/2 tbsp. (50 ml) **white wine**

Heat a little of the oil in a large saucepan over medium heat. Add the finely chopped onion and cook, stirring, over low heat for a couple of minutes; do not let the onion brown. Stir in the rice and thoroughly toast for a couple of minutes, stirring continuously. Add the wine and cook until evaporated. Raise the heat to high, adding a ladle of the hot stock at a time and stirring occasionally so that the rice does not stick to the bottom of the pot. Then add the zucchini flowers, and lastly the shrimp. When the rice is almost cooked, season with salt and stir in the butter. Continue to cook, adding the remaining stock a little at a time. Serve.

3/4 lb. (320 g) **rice**
1 lb. (400 g) **medium potatoes**
1/4 lb. (120 g) **leeks**, sliced
2 tbsp. (30 g) **butter**
1 1/2 quarts (1.5 l) **hot vegetable or meat stock**
salt and pepper

Difficulty: 1

Preparation: 10 minutes
Cooking: 20 minutes

RICE WITH POTATOES AND LEEKS

Peel the and dice the potatoes.
Melt the butter in a saucepan, and lightly cook the leeks. Add the potatoes and the rice, and then pour in the broth a little at a time. Cook, stirring frequently and adding more broth as it gradually becomes absorbed. Season to taste with salt and pepper and serve.

13 1/3 oz. (350 g) **Carnaroli rice**
3 1/2 oz. (100 g) **unsalted butter**
3 oz. (80 g) **mushrooms, thinly sliced**
3 oz. (80 g) **asparagus tips**
3 oz. (80 g) **Parma ham,** cut into julienne
3 oz. (80 g) **peeled tomatoes,** diced
1/4 cup (5 cl) **cream**
4 1/4 cups (1 l) **hot veal or beef stock**
3 oz. (80 g) grated **Parmigiano-Reggiano cheese**
1/2 **yellow onion,** chopped

Difficulty: 1

Preparation: 25 minutes
Cooking: 20 minutes

RISOTTO GIUSEPPE VERDI

Bring a pot of water to a boil, and cook the asparagus until tender. Cut off the tips and reserve; save the rest of the asparagus for another use.

Heat half of the butter in a saucepan until melted, add the onion, and lightly cook. Add the rice and cook for 1 minute. Add the mushrooms, ham, the asparagus tips, the prosciutto, and the tomatoes. Add the stock, little by little, and when the risotto is half cooked, add the cream. Continue to add the stock in increments until al dente. Stir in the rest of the butter and the Parmigiano-Reggiano, and serve.

3 1/2 oz. (100 g) **yellow onions**, chopped

1 lb. (500 g) **fava beans**, blanched and peeled if fresh, or frozen

1/3 cup plus 1 1/2 tbsp. (100 ml) **extra-virgin olive oil**

1 lb. (500 g) **chicory**

5 1/2 oz. (150 g) **crumbled stale bread**, or about 3 1/3 cups

6 1/3 cups (1.5 l) **vegetable stock** or storebought vegetable broth, heated until hot

salt

Difficulty: 1

Preparation: 10 minutes

Cooking: 50 minutes

FAVA BEAN PURÉE WITH FRIED CHICORY AND BREADCRUMBS

Heat a third of the olive oil in a pot until hot. Add the onions and cook lightly. Add the fava beans and let them cook for a few minutes; then add the hot broth. Season with salt and let the beans cook for 30 minutes until tender. Transfer to a blender and puree; the mixture will be thick.

Bring a pot of well-salted water to a boil. Blanch the chicory. Heat another third of the oil in a skillet and saute the chicory until tender. Transfer to a plate. Heat the remaining oil in the skillet. Break up the bread and fry the crumbs in the remaining oil until crispy.

Serve the chicory with the fava bean purée on the side and sprinkle the fried breadcrumbs on top.

1.1 lbs. (500 g) **eggplant**
5 1/2 oz. (150 g) **potatoes**
3 1/2 oz. (100 g) **yellow onions**, roughly chopped
1 cup (200 g) **pearl barley**
3.5 oz. (100 g) **zucchini**, diced
1 clove **garlic**
Fresh sage, thyme, and rosemary to taste
6 1/3 cups (1.5 l) **vegetable stock** or storebought vegetable broth; more as needed
salt and pepper
4 tsp. (20 ml) **extra-virgin olive oil**

Difficulty: 1

Preparation: 30 minutes
Cooking: 40 minutes

EGGPLANT PURÉE WITH ORZO AND ZUCCHINI

Peel the eggplant, reserving and thinly slicing the skin and dicing the flesh. Put the flesh in a colander, salt it lightly, and allow it to drain at least 15 minutes. Meanwhile, heat some olive oil in a pot until hot. Add the onion, garlic, and herbs and cook until the onion is tender. Add the eggplant and cook until it browns; then add the potatoes. Season with salt and pepper and pour in the stock. Continue to cook until the vegetables are tender; then transfer the vegetables and cooking liquid to a blender and purée, in batches if necessary. Return the mixture to the pot. Pour in the barley and let it cook in the vegetable purée, adding more broth if necessary. Meanwhile, in a skillet, heat the oil and sauté the zucchini until tender. Add it to the purée. In the same skillet, fry the eggplant peel. When the barley is cooked, serve the purée. Garnish with fried and finely sliced eggplant peel.

1 1/3 lb. (600 g) **potatoes**
10 1/2 oz. (300 g)
  cannarozzetti or
  spaghetti broken into
  small pieces
1 oz. (30 g) **yellow onion**,
  chopped
1.75 oz. (50 g) **carrot**, or
  about 1 small, chopped
1 oz. (30 g) **yellow onion**,
  chopped
celery, chopped
saffron threads
4 1/4 tbsp. (70 ml) **extra-
  virgin olive oil**
salt

Difficulty: 1

Preparation: 30 minutes
Cooking: 10 minutes

POTATO SOUP WITH SAFFRON

Heat the olive oil in a pot or Dutch oven. Add the onion, carrot and celery and cook lightly, stirring. Remove from the heat and let cool. Then add the saffron threads, mix well, and set aside.

Bring a saucepan of water to a boil. Cook the potatoes in the boiling water until tender, drain, and dice them.

Pour 8 1/2 cups (2 l) of water into the pot containing the saffron mixture, add the potatoes, and a little salt. Bring to a boil and then add the pasta. When the pasta is cooked, remove from the heat and let rest briefly.

This soup is also delicious without the pasta, but in this case use less water.

MARCHE-STYLE PASSATELLI

4 Servings

6 1/3 cups (1.5 l) **beef stock** or lower-salt canned beef broth
1 2/3 cups (100 g) **dried breadcrumbs**
2 large **eggs**
6 1/2 tbsp. (50 g) **all-purpose flour**
3/4 cup plus 1 tbsp. (80 g) **Parmigiano-Reggiano cheese**, grated
2 tbsp. (30 g) **unsalted butter** (optional)
2/3 cup (40 g) **fresh breadcrumbs**
salt and pepper
nutmeg, as needed
grated zest of 1/2 **lemon** (optional)

Difficulty: 1

Preparation: 40 minutes
Resting: 30 minutes
Cooking: 3-4 minutes

Combine all the ingredients except for the stock and mix until a soft dough forms. Season with salt, pepper, and ground nutmeg. Wrap the dough in plastic and refrigerate for 30 minutes.

In a saucepan, bring the stock to a boil. When it boils, pass the dough through a ricer with large holes (or a passatelli iron). Use a knife to cut the dough as it reaches a length of 1-1 1/2 inches (3-4 cm) and let the piecesfall directly into the boiling broth. Continue until all the dough has been used.

Turn the heat down to low and let the passatelli simmer for 3-4 minutes. Transfter to individual soup bowls along with the hot broth.

ITALIAN VEGETABLE SOUP

Difficulty: 1

Preparation: 1 hour
Soaking: 12 hour
Cooking: 1 hour

4 Servings

3 oz. (90 g) **leeks**, trimmed and diced
2 1/2 oz. (70 g) **celery**, diced
7 oz. (200 g) **potatoes**, peeled and diced
5 oz. (150 g) **zucchini**, diced
3 oz. (80 g) **carrots**, peeled and diced
3 1/2 oz. (100 g) **pumpkin**, trimmed, seeded, and diced
3 1/2 oz. (100 g) **dried borlotti beans**

3 1/2 oz. (100 g) **dried cannellini beans**
3 1/2 oz. (100 g) **savoy cabbage**, sliced
3 1/2 oz. (100 g) **green beans**, diced
1 bunch **fresh parsley**
1/3 cup (80 ml) **extra-virgin olive oil**
4 1/4 pints (2 l) **water**
salt
Parmigiano-Reggiano rind, as needed

Soak the borlotti and cannellini beans separately in cold water overnight.
The next day, drain the beans. Put them in a saucepan and cook the beans in cold, unsalted water until tender.
Heat 4 pints (2 liters) of water in a saucepan. In another saucepan, heat half of the oil, add the vegetables, and cook, stirring, 4-5 minutes. Then pour in the boiling water, bring to a boil, lower the heat and simmer for at least an hour, adding the drained beans toward the end of the cooking. Season with salt, if necessary, and sprinkle with parsley.
Ladle the soup into bowls, and drizzle with the remaining olive oil, a piece of Parmigiano-Reggiano rind to taste, and serve hot.

7 oz. (200 g) **dried white beans**

7 oz. (200 g) **dried cannellini beans**

7 oz. (200 g) **dried borlotti beans**

2 tbsp. (30 ml) **extra-virgin olive oil**

7 oz. (200 g) **yellow onion**

3 1/2 oz. (100 g) **carrots**, or about 2 small

3 1/2 oz. (100 g) **celery**, about 4 stalks

1 sprig **fresh thyme**, leaves removed

5 1/3 oz. (150 g) **ditalini**

salt and pepper

Difficulty: 1

Preparation: 20 minutes

Soaking: 12 hour

Cooking: 1 hour

PASTA AND BEANS

Soak the white beans, cannellini beans and the borlotti beans in cold water overnight.

The next day, drain the beans and clean and chop the onion, carrot, and celery. In a saucepan, heat the oil until hot. Add the onion, carrots, and celery and cook, stirring; then add the beans and the thyme leaves. Add enough cold water to cover and continue to cook. Ten minutes before the beans are tender, season with salt and pepper, add the ditalini and cook until the pasta is done. Transfer to individual bowls and serve.

1 lb. (500 g) **pumpkin**
(including rind)
1 1/2 lbs. (600 g) **potatoes**
3.5 oz (100 g) **yellow
onions**, sliced
7 oz. (200 g) **dried
cannellini beans**, or
about 1 cup
6 1/3 cups (1.5 l) **water**
1 sprig **fresh thyme**,
leaves minced
1 sprig **fresh rosemary**,
leaves minced
2 tsp. (10 ml) **extra-virgin
olive oil**
salt and pepper

Difficulty: 1

Preparation: 20 minutes
Soaking: 12 hour
Cooking: 45 minutes

CREAMY POTATO AND PUMPKIN SOUP
WITH CANNELLINI BEANS

Soak the cannellini beans in cold water for 12 hours or overnight.
Fill a pot with 8 1/2 cups (2 l) of water and cook the beans in the water until tender. Meanwhile, trim the pumpkin and discard the seeds. Peel the potatoes, and cut both the pumpkin and potatoes into small pieces. Put the pumpkin, potatoes, and onion in a saucepan, add enough water to cover, and bring to a boil. When the vegetables are cooked, purée them, in batches, along with the cooking liquid. Add bit of water if necessary to adjust the consistency, and season to taste with salt and pepper.
Stir the beans into the potato and pumpkin soup just before serving. Garnish with the thyme, rosemary, freshly ground pepper, and a dash of olive oil, and serve.

MAIN COURSES

THE PLEASURE GOES ON...

In Italian, the main course is called the secondo, but this is not to say that it is less important; it is the course that arrives right after the so-called primo, or first course. It is usually accompanied by a side dish made from cooked or raw vegetables, and represents the course with the most protein within an Italian-style meal—a classic main course is a serving of meat or fish. Owing to a centuries-long tradition deriving from the Christian calendar, which at one time imposed a "lean" diet based on fish for nearly half the year, Italian cuisine tends not to combine meat and fish in the same culinary preparation. And in fish recipes, animal products—such as eggs, milk, or cheese—are not used, because these fall into the category of foods to be abstained from during periods of penance.

The variety of types of fish that can be cooked is enormous, owing to the wealth of the seas surrounding the Italian peninsula and the numerous rivers and lakes punctuating the inlands. For as many species as there are, both freshwater and saltwater, there are as many recipes that have, over the centuries, brought out their best. Today, fish—enjoyed in recipes of great simplicity and lightness, like Swordfish with Lemon and Capers, or in more extravagant preparations, like the Mixed Fried Fish—is turning into the star of Italian cooking. This may also be for its attractive nutritional benefits, making it one of the key foods in the Mediterranean diet, which is now increasingly recommended by nutritionists for maintaining good health.

The choice among meats and their culinary possibilities is equally broad. When it comes to poultry, the most highly appreciated is still the chicken, which appears in so many typical Italian recipes. Up until just a short while ago, a roast chicken with potatoes and a salad from the garden was the symbolic Sunday lunch for Italians. While beef is has a stronger flavor, veal is also highly appreciated, with its white meat and soft and delicate flavor, as is pork, which has always been used to prepare delicious recipes as well as excellent sausages and cured meats. Not to mention the love of meats that are closer to nature, such as game meats—deemed so delicious that up until the beginning of the 20th century they were the triumph of the noble banquets—or lamb and goat meat, which make their appearance in central Italy as highlights of the Easter table.

LOBSTER TAIL WITH TOMATO CONFIT AND BASIL OIL

4 SERVINGS

24 small **lobster tails**
1 oz. (30 g) **fresh basil**, or about 1 1/4 cups whole leaves
3.5 oz. (100 g) **mixed greens**, for serving
3 tbsp. (40 ml) **extra-virgin olive oil**

FOR THE TOMATO CONFIT
2 1/2 lbs. (1.2 kg) **ripe tomatoes**, or about 6 1/2 large
1 clove **garlic**, thinly sliced
1/2 oz. (10 g) **fresh thyme**, or about 1/4 cup
2 tsp. (10 ml) **extra-virgin olive oil**
sugar
salt and pepper

Shell the lobster tails, using scissors to cut down the back. Season with salt, pepper and some of the oil and let them marinate.

Heat the oven to 175°F (80°C) and line a baking sheet with parchment.

Have ready a bowl of ice water. Bring a saucepan of water to a boil. Peel the tomatoes, drop them in the boiling water, and blanch them for 30 seconds. Transfer them immediately to the ice water. Cut them into quarters, remove the seeds, and lay the tomatoes on the baking sheet. Season on both sides with the thyme, garlic, and a pinch each of salt, pepper and sugar. Bake for 1 hour.

Line another pan with parchment and set four individual square cooking molds on it. Fill them with alternating layers of the tomatoes and lobster tails, finishing with a layer of tomatoes. Raise the oven temperature to 300°F (150°C), transfer to the oven, and bake for 6 minutes.

Have ready a bowl of ice water. Bring a small saucepan of water to a boil and blanch the basil leaves, 2 minutes. Strain and put them directly in the ice water. Return the basil leaves to the pan and use an immersion blender to blend them with the remaining oil.

Remove the molds from the oven and serve the lobster tails and tomatoes with the basil oil, along with the mixed greens.

Difficulty: 2

Preparation: 1 hour 30 minutes

Cooking: 6 minutes

2 1/4 lbs. (1 kg) **mussels**, scrubbed and debearded
1 clove **garlic**
4 tbsp. (60 ml) **extra-virgin olive oil**
8 slices **crusty bread**, toasted (optional)
fresh parsley, chopped, to taste
pepper

Difficulty: 1

Preparation: 20 minutes
Cooking: 5 minutes

PEPPERED MUSSELS

Heat the oil in a skillet. Add the whole clove of garlic and cook until fragrant, but do not brown.

Add the mussels, cover, and cook until they open.

Discard any mussels that have not opened. Sprinkle the mussels generously with freshly ground pepper and parsley. Stir well. Transfer to serving bowls. Serve with the toasted bread, if using.

SQUID WITH PEAS

4 SERVINGS

1 3/4 lbs. (800 g) **squid**
5 1/2 oz. (150 g) **yellow onions**, chopped
1 clove **garlic**, chopped
1 bunch **fresh basil**, sliced
1/3 cup plus 1 1/2 tbsp. (100 ml) **extra-virgin olive oil**
1 tbsp. minced **fresh parsley**
5 1/2 oz. (150 g) **tomato purée**
1/3 cup plus 1 1/2 tbsp. (100 ml) **white wine**
5 1/2 oz. (160 g) **peas**, or about 1 cup
salt and pepper

Difficulty: 1

Preparation: 20 minutes
Cooking: 40 minutes

Clean the squid by removing the skin from the body and cutting the tentacles from the body. Flip back the tentacles and squeeze out and discard the beak located in the center of the tentacles. Remove the eyes, the entrails, and the transparent inner cartilage. Cut the body of the squid into rings.
Heat the oil in a saucepan over medium heat. Add the onion and sauté. Add the squid and the garlic and let cook for a couple of minutes. Pour in the white wine and let it evaporate. Add the tomato purée, peas, parsley, and basil. Season with a pinch each of salt and pepper and cook until the squid is very tender. Serve.

1 lb. 6 oz. (650 g) **baccalà**
   (dried cod)
10 1/2 oz. (300 g)
   potatoes
pinch saffron
1 tbsp. chopped **fresh**
   parsley
1 **bay leaf**
5 tbsp. (70 g) **unsalted**
   butter
cayenne
salt

Difficulty: 1

Preparation: 40 minutes
Cooking: 10 minutes

BACCALÀ WITH POTATOES AND SAFFRON

Peel the potatoes and use a small knife to give them a regular shape. In a saucepan, bring a little over 1 quart (1 l) well-salted water, the saffron, and the bay leaf to a boil. Cook the potatoes in the boiling water until they are tender but maintain a bit of their consistency. Keep warm in the cooking water.
Meanwhile, cut the cod into slices and season with salt. Melt the butter and cayenne as desired in a skillet and cook, turning over halfway through cooking and sprinkling with some of the parsley toward the end, about 10 minutes.
Drain the potatoes, cut them into thick rounds, and distribute them on individual plates. Arrange the slices of cod on the potatoes, garnish with cayenne and parsley, and serve.

3 lbs. 5 oz. (1.5 kg) **sea bass**
5 1/2 oz. (150 g) **yellow onion**, about 1 medium, thinly sliced
1/2 lb. (250 g) **cherry tomatoes**
3 1/2 tbsp. (50 ml) **extra-virgin olive oil**
5 fresh **basil leaves**
2 cloves **garlic**
3/4 cup plus 1 1/2 tbsp (200 ml) **water**
salt and pepper

Difficulty: 1

Preparation: 15 minutes
Cooking: 20 minutes

SEA BASS IN *ACQUA PAZZA* ("CRAZY WATER")

Clean and fillet the sea bass, removing all the bones.
Heat the olive oil in a skillet until hot. Sauté the onion, garlic, and basil, and then add the tomatoes and water; let cook for about 10 minutes. Season the fish with salt and pepper, then add it to the acqua pazza and let it cook through. Serve.

2 **sea bass** (1 1/3 lbs. or 500-600 g each), filleted

7 oz. (200 g) **potatoes**

1 oz. (28 g) **capers in salt**, rinsed

3 oz. (80 g) **Taggiasca olives**

1/3 cup plus 1 1/2 tbsp. (100 ml) **extra-virgin olive oil**

1 tbsp. chopped **fresh parsley**

a few sprigs **fresh rosemary**

a few **fresh sage** leaves

salt and pepper

Difficulty 2

Difficulty: 2

Preparation: 20 minutes

Cooking: 12-15 minutes

SEA BASS BAKED IN PARCHMENT WITH POTATOES, CAPERS, AND OLIVES

Bring a pot of well-salted water to a boil. Peel the potatoes and cut them into wedges. Cook them in the salted water for 5 minutes, then drain.

Heat the oven to 350°F(180°C). Season the sea bass fillets with salt and pepper and place them in on sheets of parchment. Evenly distribute the olives, capers, and potato wedges over each fillet, along with the sprigs of rosemary and sage leaves. Drizzle with the oil and seal the packets.

Wrap the packets individually in aluminum foil and bake for 12 to 15 minutes. Serve the fillets sprinkled with the parsley.

1 lb. 2 oz. (500 g) **sea bass**
4 tbsp. (60 ml) **extra-virgin olive oil**
3 1/2 oz. (100 g) **green olives**, about 24 large
7 oz. (200 g) **cherry tomatoes**, halved, or about 1 cup
2 tbsp. (20 g) **capers**, rinsed
fresh parsley
salt and pepper

Difficulty: 1

Preparation: 20 minutes
Cooking: 15 minutes

SEA BASS WITH CHERRY TOMATOES, CAPERS, AND OLIVES

Clean and skin the sea bass, then wash and fillet. Put the fillets in a lightly oiled pan. Add the tomatoes, season with salt and pepper, and add the capers. Drizzle with the remaining oil, cover, and cook for 15 minutes over low heat (you can also cook in a medium-hot oven), adding a little water if necessary. Towards the end of cooking, add the olives and sprinkle a little chopped parsley on top. Serve.

GROUPER MATALOTTA-STYLE

Difficulty: 1

Preparation: 25 minutes

Cooking: 15 minutes

4 Servings

1 3/4 lb. (800 g) **grouper fillets**
1/2 cup (60 g) **all-purpose flour**
7 oz. (200 g) **tomatoes**, quartered
3 1/2 oz. (100 g) **yellow onion**, julienned
1/2 oz. (5 g) **garlic** or about 1 clove,
thinly sliced
1 **bay leaf**
1/2 oz. (8 g) **fresh parsley**, chopped
1/2 cup (100 ml) **white wine**
3 1/2 tbsp. (50 ml) **extra-virgin olive oil**
salt and pepper

1/2 cup (100 ml) **fish stock**
3 1/2 oz. (100 g) **button mushrooms**,
sliced

FOR THE GARNISH
3 1/2 oz. (100 g) **zucchini**, sliced
4 tbsp. (60 ml) **extra-virgin olive oil**
3 oz. (80 g) **bell peppers**, cut into 2/3
in. (2 cm) pieces
1/4 cup (30 g) **sliced almonds**

Put some of the flour in a shallow tray. Dredge the grouper fillets in the flour. Heat the oil in a skillet until hot. Sauté the onion and the garlic for 1 minute. Add the fish fillets and fry gently. Add the white wine and simmer until it evaporates. Add the tomatoes, season with salt and pepper, and add the fish broth, bay leaf, mushrooms, and parsley and cook over low heat for 5 minutes.

In a separate skillet, sauté the sliced zucchini. Add the peppers, season with salt, and sauté over high heat. Add the almonds.

Remove the bay leaf. Arrange the fillets on a serving dish, then garnish with the vegetables.

1 lb. (450 g) **squid**
9 oz. (250 g) **red mullet**
7 oz. (200 g) **prawns**
3 1/2 oz. (100 g) **anchovies**
5 oz. (150 g) **sardines**
2/3 cup (100 g) **semolina flour**
Oil for frying as needed
salt

Difficulty: 2

Preparation: 30 minutes
Cooking: 5 minutes

MIXED FRIED FISH

Clean the squid by removing the skin from the body and cutting the tentacles from the body. Flip back the tentacles and squeeze out and discard the beak located in the center of the tentacles. Remove the eyes, the entrails, and the transparent inner cartilage. Cut the body of the squid into rings (if the squid is small, it can even be left whole).

Prepare and fillet the red mullet, gut the anchovies and sardines, and clean the prawns, removing the heads.

Heat the oil in a large skillet until hot. Dip the various types of fish in the semolina flour and fry them separately, making sure that the oil does not overheat.

Remove the fish from the oil with a skimmer and dry on paper towels. Season with a pinch of salt and serve.

1 **sea bream** or sea bass, 2 lbs., 3 oz. (1 kg)
10 1/2 oz. (300 g) **potatoes**
2 oz. (50 g) **Pecorino cheese**, grated, or about 1/2 cup
1 clove **garlic**, minced
1 tbsp. chopped **fresh parsley**
3 tbsp. (40 ml) **extra-virgin olive oil**
salt and pepper

Difficulty: 1

Preparation: 30 minutes
Cooking: 15-20 minutes

PUGLIA-STYLE SEA BREAM

Clean, scale and fillet the fish.
Bring a pot of well-salted water to a boil. Peel the potatoes, slice them very thinly and blanch them in the boiling water.
Heat the oven to 400°F (200°C). Grease a baking pan (or line it with parchment paper) and cover the bottom with a layer of potatoes. Combine the Pecorino, garlic, and parsley and sprinkle half of the mixture evenly over the potatoes. Top with a layer of sea bream fillets and sprinkle them with salt and pepper. Cover them with the other half of the Pecorino mixture, and then the potatoes, being careful to place the potato slices gently.
Drizzle with the extra-virgin olive oil and bake for 15-20 minutes. Serve.

SWORDFISH STEAK
WITH LEMON AND CAPERS

Difficulty: 1

Preparation: 20 minutes

Cooking: 10 minutes

4 SERVINGS

14 oz. (400 g) **swordfish steaks**
1 oz. (25 g) **capers packed in salt**, or about 3 tbsp., rinsed well
5 1/2 oz. (150 g) **mache**
2 **lemons**
7 tbsp. (103.5 ml) **extra-virgin olive oil**
salt and pepper

Heat the oven to 350°F (180°C) and grease a baking dish with extra-virgin olive oil. Slice the swordfish into 4 pieces. Season with salt and pepper on both sides and arrange the fish in the baking dish.

Remove the peel and pith from one of the lemons. Working over a bowl to catch the juices, use a paring knife to slice between the sections and membranes of each fruit; remove the segments whole, reserving the fruit and juice. Dice the lemon segments. Cover the swordfish with the diced lemon and capers. Pour the lemon juice on top and drizzle with 4 tbsp. (60 ml) extra-virgin olive oil. Transfer to the oven and bake, covering with foil if it gets too dry.

Juice the second lemon, and in a bowl, combine the juice with the 3 tbs. (43.5 ml) oil; season with salt and pepper to taste.

Combine the mache with the lemon dressing and serve with the swordfish.

MONKFISH IN LEEK SAUCE
WITH ITALIAN OLIVES

Difficulty: 1

Preparation: 40 minutes
Cooking: 25 minutes

4 Servings

3 1/3 lb. (1.5 kg) **monkfish**
5 tbsp. (70 ml) **extra-virgin olive oil**
7 oz. (200 g) **ripe tomatoes**, halved
1 lb. 2 oz. (500 g) **leeks**
2 cloves **garlic**, sliced
1 bunch **fresh parsley**, chopped
1 lb. 2 oz. (500 g) **olives**
3 cups (700 ml) **water**
4 tsp. (20 ml) **white vinegar**
crushed red pepper flakes
salt and freshly ground pepper

Remove the head, skin and tail from the monkfish and wash it carefully.
Using a sharp knife, fillet the fish and remove the central bone to obtain two fillets.
Trim the leeks, remove and discard the dark green parts, and slice the white and light green parts into rounds. Rinse well under running water.
Bring a saucepan of well-salted water to a boil. Blanch the leeks in water and vinegar for a few seconds, drain and dry.
Bring another pot of well-salted water to a boil. Cut the monkfish fillets into uniform pieces, blanch for a few minutes, drain, and set aside.
Heat the oil in a skillet over medium heat. Add the leeks and garlic and cook until softened. Add a pinch of chile flakes, the tomatoes, and the parsley, and bring to a boil. Add the monkfish and the olives. Lower the heat to low and cook for 15 minutes. Season with salt and freshly ground pepper and serve.

ALMOND AND PISTACHIO-CRUSTED AMBERJACK STEAK WITH ARTICHOKE SALAD

Difficulty: 1

Preparation: 40 minutes
Cooking: 5-10 minutes

4 Servings

1 lb. (500 g) **amberjack steaks** or mahi mahi
1 1/2 oz. (40 g) **capers**, or about 4 1/2 tbsp.
3 1/2 oz. (100 g) **blanched almonds**, or about 1 cup chopped
3 1/2 oz. (100 g) **pistachios**, or about 3/4 cup whole
1 lb. 5 oz. (600 g) **artichokes**
1 bunch **fresh mint**, finely chopped
2 **lemons**
1/3 cup plus 1 1/2 tbsp. (100 ml) **extra-virgin olive oil**
salt and pepper

Heat the oven to 350°F (180°C).
Juice the lemons, and add half of the juice to a bowl of water. Remove the tough outer leaves from the artichokes. Cut them in half and remove and discard the chokes. Slice the artichokes very thinly and put them in the lemon water to prevent discoloration.
Crush the pistachios and almonds and spread them in a shallow dish. Cut the fish crosswise into thick slices and coat them in the crushed nuts.
In a blender, blend the capers with 3 1/2 tbsp. (50 ml) of the extra-virgin olive oil and reserve.
In a heatproof skillet, heat a quarter of the remaining oil over medium heat. Sear the fish over medium heat, season with salt and transfer to the oven. Bake for 5-10 minutes, depending on the size of the slices.
Drain the artichokes and toss them with the remaining lemon juice, the remaining oil, and the mint, and season to taste with salt and pepper.
Serve the fish with the artichoke salad and caper oil.

1 1/3 lbs. (600 g) **salmon fillet**
1 lb. (400 g) **potatoes**
2 large **eggs**
1 tbsp. chopped **fresh parsley**
3 1/2 tbsp. (50 g) **unsalted butter**
salt and pepper

Difficulty: 1

Preparation: 30 minutes
Cooking: 7-8 minutes

SALMON WITH POTATOES AND EGGS

Bring a small saucepan of water to a boil. Cook the eggs, about 10 minutes. Run under cold water to cool. Peel and press the eggs through a sieve. Set aside.
Bring a pot of well-salted water to a boil. Peel the potatoes, and using a corer with a diameter of 2.5 cm (1 in), make little potato balls. Cook the potato balls in the boiling water for 5 minutes.
Cut the salmon into 4 fillets and season with salt and pepper.
Melt the butter in a skillet and when it begins to foam, brown the salmon on both sides. Add the potatoes and bake in the oven at 350°F (180°C) for 7 to 8 minutes. Transfer the salmon and potatoes to plates, and sprinkle with parsley and the sieved eggs.

17 1/2 oz. (500 g) **sardines**
3 1/2 oz. (100 g)
   breadcrumbs, or about
   1 cup
2 **salt-packed anchovies**
1 oz. (20 g) **pine nuts**, or
   about 2 tbsp.
1 oz. (20 g) **raisins**
1 tbsp. chopped **fresh
   parsley**
3 1/2 tbsp. (50 ml) **extra-
   virgin olive oil**
fresh bay leaves, as
   needed
salt and pepper

Difficulty: 2

Preparation: 30 minutes
Cooking: 7-8 minutes

BECCAFICO SARDINES

Prepare the sardines, removing the heads and the insides. Remove the bones but leave the tail intact. Rinse and bone the sardines, then chop them finely. Soak the raisins in a bowl of lukewarm water for 15 minutes, then drain and press to remove excess water. Heat three-quarters of the oil in a skillet and pour in the breadcrumbs. Sauté until they start to brown. Transfer to a bowl to cool, and then add the parsley, pine nuts, raisins and anchovies. Season with salt and pepper and mix well.
Heat the oven to 350°F (180°C) and oil a baking pan.
Cut the sardines lengthwise and open them up like a book, skin side down. Put a little of the breadcrumb mixture in each sardine and then roll them up, starting from the head end so that the tail is left outside. Secure the rolls with a cocktail stick. Arrange the bay leaves in the prepared pan and place the sardines on the bay leaves. Drizzle with the remaining oil and bake for about 20 minutes.

DUCK BREASTS WITH HONEY

Difficulty: 2

Preparation: 20 minutes
Cooking: 15 minutes

4 SERVINGS

2 **boneless duck breasts**
2 oz. (50 g) **yellow onion**, chopped
1 clove **garlic**
3 tbsp. (approx. 60 g) **honey**
Fresh **rosemary, sage and bay leaf**, as needed
salt and pepper

Heat the oven to 350°F (180°C).
Score the skin and fat on each duck breast without cutting into the meat, and season with salt and pepper. Heat a skillet until hot and cook the duck, skin side down first, until crisp. Transfer the duck breasts to a baking pan, and add the garlic clove, the onion and the herbs. Roast for about 10 minutes; the duck breasts should still be soft and pink inside.
Let them rest for a few minutes, covered in tin foil, before slicing.
Spoon the fat from the baking pan and then add the honey. When you have obtained the desired thickness, strain the sauce through a sieve.
Serve the duck breasts, covered with the honey sauce.

CHICKEN STUFFED WITH CHESTNUTS

Difficulty: 3

Preparation: 1 hour
Cooking: 1 hour

4 SERVINGS

1 approximately 2 lb. 3 oz. (1 kg) **chicken**
14 oz. (400 g) **sausage**
3 1/2 oz. (100 g) **chestnuts**, cooked and peeled
1 large **egg**
7 oz. (200 g) **yellow onion**, diced
5 oz. (150 g) **carrots**, diced
3 oz. (80 g) **celery**, diced
2 cloves **garlic**
Fresh **rosemary, thyme, bay leaf, and sage**, to taste
nutmeg, to taste
salt and pepper

Remove the chicken's breastbone and season the inside of the chicken with salt and pepper.
To prepare the stuffing, remove the casing from the sausage put the sausage meat in a bowl. Add the egg and a pinch of nutmeg and knead the mixture together. Season with salt and pepper.
Bring a saucepan of water to a boil. Boil the chestnuts, drain, and let cool before peeling, taking care not to break them. Add them to the stuffing.
Heat the oven to 350°F (180°C).
Stuff the chicken with the stuffing and close the breast opening using a kitchen needle and twine.
Sauté the the chicken in a heavy-duty baking pan, then add the onion, carrots, celery, herbs, and garlic cloves. Transfer to the oven and roast the bird for 50 minutes to an hour. If necessary, add a little water.
As soon as the chicken is cooked, tent with foil and set aside.
Deglaze and strain the pan juices. Carve the chicken and serve with the pan juices.

2 lbs. 3 oz. (1 kg) **guinea fowl**
7 oz. (200 g) **cabbage**
5 oz. (150 g) **porcini mushrooms**
1/3 cup plus 1 1/2 tbsp. (100 ml) **white wine**
1 sprig **fresh rosemary**
2 cloves **garlic**
3 1/2 tbsp. (50 ml) **extra-virgin olive oil**
1 tbsp. minced **fresh parsley**
salt and pepper

Difficulty: 2

Preparation: 20 minutes
Cooking: 50 minutes

BRAISED GUINEA FOWL

Heat the oven to 350°F (180°C). Season the outside of the guinea fowl with salt, rub with some of the oil, and put the the rosemary and garlic inside the cavity. Put the guinea fowl in a baking pan and roast for 30 minutes. Bring a saucepan of well-salted water to a boil. Blanch the cabbage in the boiling water for 3 to 4 minutes. Drain and reserve the cooking water. Roughly chop the cabbage, and clean and dice the mushrooms. Heat a bit of the oil in a skillet until hot. Add the mushrooms, the remaining clove garlic, and the rosemary, and sauté. Add the cabbage, season with salt and pepper, and let cook for a few minutes. Pour in some of the cabbage cooking water. When the guinea fowl is done, remove it from the oven and cut it into 8 pieces. Transfer to the pan of vegetables and let everything stew for about 20 minutes. To serve, transfer to individual plates, sprinkle each serving with freshly ground black pepper, and drizzle with extra-virgin olive oil.

1 **chicken**
1/3 cup plus 1 1/2 tbsp. (100 ml) **extra-virgin olive oil**
9 oz. (250 g) **red bell pepper**, or 2 medium
9 oz. (250 g) **yellow bell pepper**, or 2 medium
3.5 oz. (100 g) **yellow onion**, sliced
3/4 cup plus 1 1/2 tbsp. (200 ml) **Marsala wine**
1 1/4 cups (300 ml) **chicken stock**
flour, as needed
cornstarch, as needed
1 sprig **fresh rosemary**
salt and pepper

Difficulty: 1

Preparation: 30 minutes
Cooking: 30 minutes

CHICKEN MARSALA WITH PEPPERS

Cut the chicken into pieces and season with salt and pepper. Put the flour in a shallow dish and coat the lightly with flour.

Slice the bell peppers into small strips.

Heat two-thirds of the oil in a skillet until hot. Brown the chicken pieces and transfer to a plate.

Add the remaining oil to the skillet, and sauté the onion and rosemary. Return the chicken to the skillet, pour in the Marsala, and let it evaporate. Add the peppers to the pan. Let everything finish cooking, occasionally adding stock as needed and seasoning with salt and pepper to taste.

If you prefer a thicker sauce, dissolve a pinch of cornstarch in a few drops of water and stir it in at the very end.

BEEF BRAISED IN BAROLO WINE

Difficulty: 3

Preparation: 30 minutes
Marinating: 12 hours
Cooking: 3 hours

4 SERVINGS

3 1/3 lbs. (1.5 kg) **beef chuck**
1 bottle **Barolo wine**
3 1/2 tbsp. (50 ml) **extra-virgin olive oil**
2 cloves **garlic**, chopped
2 1/2 oz. (75 g) **yellow onion**, diced
2 oz. (60 g) **carrot**, diced
2 **stalks celery**, diced

1 sprig **fresh rosemary**
1 bunch **fresh sage**
1 **bay leaf**
1 **clove**
1 **cinnamon stick**
3-4 **peppercorns**
salt

Tie the beef with kitchen twine and put it in a bowl with the spices, herbs and vegetables.

Add the Barolo and marinate the refrigerator for 12 hours. Remove the meat and dry it. Strain out the vegetables, reserving the vegetables and the marinade.

Heat the oil in a Dutch oven and sear the meat. Add the reserved vegetables and continue to cook; then add the reserved marinade, season with salt, cover, and cook on low heat.

When the meat is cooked, remove it from the Dutch oven and let cool so that it is easier to slice. Meanwhile, put the sauce through a vegetable mill (or blend in a food processor), strain it in a sieve, and if necessary, reduce.

Slice the beef into thick slices and immerse them in the sauce. Leave them there for a while to acquire flavor before serving.

CRUSTED VEAL TENDERLOIN

Difficulty: 1

Preparation: 20 minutes
Cooking: 5-7 minutes

4 Servings

1 lb. (400 g) **yukon gold potatoes**
1 lb. 5 oz. (600 g) **veal tenderloin**
2 1/2 tbsp. (35 ml) **extra-virgin olive oil**
fresh thyme
salt and pepper

Heat the oven to 400°F (200°C) and line a baking sheet with parchment.
Peel the potatoes and slice them on a mandolin with a waffle-cut blade, rotating them 90° between one cut and the next to produce potato "grilles." Soak in running cold water.
Trim the veal fillet of its fat and cut it into four medallions.
Heat three-quarters of the extra-virgin olive oil in a skillet with the thyme. Remove the thyme, then sear the medallions, quickly browning them on both sides. Season with salt and pepper.
Arrange some of the potato "grilles" on the baking sheet. Overlap the fillets, covering with the remaining potatoes.
Season lightly with salt, drizzle with the remaining extra-virgin olive oil, and roast for 5 to 7 minutes.

1 3/4 lbs. (800 g) **beef chuck**
1 lb. (400 g) **yellow onions, chopped**
3/4 cup plus 2 tbsp. (200 ml) **red wine**
1 tsp. **paprika**
1 oz. (25 g) **all-purpose flour**, or about 3 tbsp.
1 strip **lemon zest**
1 sprig **fresh rosemary**
1 **bay leaf**
1 sprig **fresh marjoram**
2 tbsp. (30 ml) **olive oil**
1 oz. (30 g) **tomato paste**
salt and pepper

Difficulty: 1

Preparation: 25

Cooking: 2 hours
15 minutes

VAL PUSTERIA-STYLE GOULASH

Cut the meat into cubes. Heat the oil in a skillet until hot, add the meat and the onions, and sauté for a few minutes.

Dissolve the flour and the paprika in a little water in a glass and pour over the meat. Pour in half of the red wine and simmer until it evaporates. Add the rosemary, bay, marjoram, the lemon zest, and the tomato paste and mix well. Add a glass of water and the remaining wine; cover and let cook, at least 2 hours. If the dish becomes too dry during cooking, add a little water.

Before serving, remove the bay leaf. Serve the goulash with polenta, boiled potatoes or flour dumplings.

1 lb. 2 oz. (500 g) **plum tomatoes**, diced
8 **veal escalopes**, about 2 oz. (60 g) each
4 tbsp. (60 ml) **extra-virgin olive oil**
4 1/2 tbsp. (40 g) **capers**, rinsed
8 **slices sandwich bread** (optional)
flour, as needed
oregano
salt

Difficulty: 1

Preparation: 30 minutes
Cooking: 10 minutes

VEAL ESCALOPES ALLA PIZZAIOLA

Cut the crusts off the slices of sandwich bread and toast them in the oven or on the grill, if using.

Trim the escalopes, pound them lightly with a meat mallet, and dredge in flour.

In a skillet, heat the oil until hot. Add the escalopes and cook them quickly on both sides. Season with salt and keep warm.

To the same pan, add the tomatoes and cook over high heat for 5 minutes. Season to taste with salt, and add a little oregano and the capers. Return the escalopes to the pan and to finish cooking.

Serve on crostini, if using.

ROAST WHOLE VEAL SHANK

Difficulty: 1

Preparation: 20 minutes

Cooking: 1 hour

4 SERVINGS

2 2/3 lbs. (1.2 kg) **veal shank**
2 oz. (50 g) **lard** or bacon fat
1/2 oz. (10 g) **fresh rosemary**
extra-virgin olive oil, as needed
3 oz. (80 g) **yellow onion**, diced
2 oz. (60 g) **carrot**, diced
1 1/2 oz. (40 g) **celery**, diced
1 cup (200 ml) **white wine**
1/2 cup (100 g) **crushed tomatoes**
veal stock, as needed
garlic to taste
salt and pepper

Trim the excess fat from the veal shank, make deep slits all over the meat and season with salt and pepper.

Make a mixture of crushed garlic, rosemary, and lard and insert it into the slits in the meat.

Heat the oil in a Dutch oven and brown the meat over medium heat, then add the diced onion, carrot and celery.

Sauté, then splash with the white wine and cook until it evaporates. Add the tomato pulp.

Roast in the oven at a 350°F (180°C); add stock if necessary during cooking.

When the meat is cooked, let the sauce simmer and, if necessary, thicken with a little cornstarch dissolved in a spoonful of water.

TUSCAN STYLE ROAST LOIN OF PORK

Difficulty: 1

Preparation: 30 minutes

Cooking: 1 hour

4 SERVINGS

1 **pork loin**, about 2 1/4 lbs. (1 kg), on the bone
2 cloves **garlic**, chopped
2 sprigs **rosemary**, leaves chopped
7 tbsp. (100 ml) **extra-virgin olive oil**
salt and pepper

Heat the oven to 350°F (180°C).
Partially separate the bones from the joint of meat without removing the bone.
Make a mixture of the garlic, rosemary, a generous pinch of salt, and a pinch of pepper. Distribute half of the mixture between the bone and the meat. Then tie the two parts together with kitchen twine. Spread the rest of the garlic and rosemary mixture all over the outside of the meat, massaging well.
Put the meat in a baking pan. Drizzle with the oil, transfer to the oven and roast for about an hour.
When the meat is cooked, remove the twine and the bone and slice the meat. Serve with the pan juices.

2 **pork tenderloins**, 1 lb. 10
   oz. (750 g)
5 oz. (150 g) **Parma ham**
Balsamic Vinegar of
   Modena, to taste
1 sprig **fresh rosemary**
2 cloves **garlic**
10 oz. (300 g) **baby salad**
   greens
extra-virgin olive oil
salt and pepper

Difficulty: 1

Preparation: 20 minutes
Cooking: 10 minutes

PORK TENDERLOIN WITH HAM
AND BALSAMIC VINEGAR OF MODENA

Trim the excess fat from the slices of ham. Cut the pork into small pieces, about
2 oz. (60 g) each. Wrap each piece of pork in a slice of ham, fixing it in place with
a toothpick. Heat a little olive oil in a skillet; add the rosemary and the garlic and
the pieces of pork. Drizzle the meat with the balsamic vinegar according to your
taste, and cook on both sides until the center is no longer pink. Before serving,
place the meat on a bed of the greens and season with salt, freshly ground black
pepper and olive oil. Pour over the reduced balsamic vinegar sauce.

1 lb. 2 oz. (500 g) **pork tenderloin**
3 1/2 oz. (100 g) **caul fat**
2 oz. (50 g) **lard** or bacon fat
1/2 clove **garlic**
2 1/4 tbsp. (30 ml) **extra-virgin olive oil**
10 tsp. (50 g) **unsalted butter**
1/3 cup plus 1 1/2 tbsp. (100 ml) **Marsala wine**
2 oz. (50 g) **Parma ham**, sliced
fresh sage, chopped , to taste
fresh rosemary, chopped, to taste
fresh thyme, chopped, to taste
flour, as needed
salt and pepper

Difficulty: 2

Preparation: 30 minutes
Cooking: 15 minutes

PORK TENDERLOIN IN MARSALA WINE

Rinse the caul fat under running water.
Prepare a mixture of lard, sage, rosemary, thyme and garlic.
Trim any excess fat off the pork tenderloin, season with salt and pepper, and spread the mixture of lard and herbs over it. Wrap it in the Parma ham and then in the caul fat. Flour the pork lightly. Heat the oil and butter in the skillet, add the pork, and sauté, then add the bits of fat that you have trimmed off and roast in the oven at 400°F (200°C) for 12-13 minutes. As soon as it is cooked, remove the pork from the pan and keep warm. Spoon out the excess fat, deglaze the baking pan with the Marsala wine, and reduce the pan juices as necessary.
Slice the meat and serve with the sauce.

WILD BOAR WITH POLENTA

Difficulty: 3

Preparation: 30 minutes
Marinating: 12 hours
Cooking: 3 hours

4 Servings

FOR THE WILD BOAR
2 lbs. 10 oz. (1.2 kg) **wild boar**, lean cut
1 bottle red wine
3 1/2 tbsp. (50 ml) **extra-virgin olive oil**
2 cloves **garlic**
2 1/2 oz. (75 g) **yellow onions**, about 1/2
medium, diced
2 oz. (60 g) **carrot**, diced
2 **stalks celery**, diced
1 sprig **fresh rosemary**
1 **bunch sage**
1 **bay leaf**
1 **clove**

1 **cinnamon stick**
3-4 **peppercorns**
3-4 **juniper berries**
1 **liqueur glass grappa**
1 tbsp. **tomato paste**
salt to taste

FOR THE POLENTA
2 cups (500 ml) **water**
3 1/2 oz. (100 g) **corn meal flour**
4 tbsp. (20 g) **unsalted butter**
salt

Dice the wild boar into 1 in. (3-4 cm) cubes and put them in a bowl with the spices, herbs, a whole clove of garlic and the washed, dried, diced vegetables. Add the red wine and marinate in the refrigerator for 12 hours. Drain the meat and dry it, reserving the vegetables and marinade.

Heat the oil in a saucepan and cook the meat, along with the other whole clove of garlic. Add the vegetables and continue to cook. Pour in the Grappa and then the marinade. Season with salt, add the tomato paste, cover, and cook on low heat.

When the meat is cooked, remove it from the saucepan. Pass the sauce through a food mill (or blend in a food processor), strain it in a sieve and, if necessary, reduce. Return the meat back to the sauce and leave it there to acquire flavor.

Meanwhile, prepare the polenta: bring a pan (preferable copper) of well-salted water to a boil. Pour the cornmeal flour in a steady stream into the boiling water, along with together with 1 tbsp. of the butter. Cook the polenta for about half an hour, stirring frequently with a wooden spoon. Stir in the remaining butter.

Serve the wild boar with freshly cooked soft polenta or, if you prefer, polenta in slices known as "crostoni." (To make crostoni, pour the cooked polenta into an oiled baking pan, spread it to a thickness of 1/2 to 3/4 in. (1-2 cm) and let cool completely. Cut it into the shapes of your choice and brown in the oven or on a griddle.)

1 lb. 12 oz. (800 g) **lamb**
2 lbs. 10 1/2 oz. (1.2 kg) **potatoes**
2 cloves **garlic**
2 sprigs **fresh thyme**
1 oz. (30 g) **fresh rosemary**, or about 1/2 cup plus 1 tbsp.
2/3 cup (150 ml) **extra-virgin olive oil**
salt and pepper

Difficulty: 1

Preparation: 50 minutes
Cooking: 10 minutes

GRILLED LAMB SKEWERS WITH THYME

Heat the oven to 350°F (180°C). Soak wooden skewers in water for 20 minutes. Cut the lamb into 1/3-3/4 inch (1-2 cm) cubes and slide them onto the skewers.
Bring a pot of water to a boil. Peel the potatoes and cut them into wedges. Cook them for 5 minutes, drain, and put them in a preheated baking dish with half of the oil, 1 of the garlic cloves, salt and pepper. Roast for 30 minutes.
Strip the thyme from the stem and thinly slice the remaining garlic clove. Spread them over the skewers and drizzle the remaining olive oil on top. Let the meat marinate for at least 20-30 minutes in the refrigerator.
Before grilling, let the skewers warm up to room temperature for about 10 minutes, and remove the garlic and thyme from the meat to prevent them from burning. Cook the skewers on a grill or flat griddle for about 10 minutes, seasoning with salt and pepper to taste. Serve with the potato wedges.

5 1/2 lbs. (2.5 kg) **leg of lamb**, bone-in
3 1/2 tbsp. (50 ml) **extra-virgin olive oil**
2 cloves **garlic**
fresh thyme, chopped, as needed
fresh rosemary, chopped, as needed
salt and pepper

Difficulty: 2

Preparation: 20 minutes
Cooking: 4 hours

ROAST LEG OF LAMB

It's an Italian tradition to roast lamb in a bed of hay, which helps keep the meat moist. But since hay isn't widely available to American cooks, this version of the recipe omits it, relying instead on slow cooking for succulent flavor and texture.
Bone the leg of lamb. Put half of the herbs on the inside, along with 1 clove of the garlic, and season with salt and pepper. Roll the leg back up and tie with kitchen twine. Heat the oven to 350°F (180°C). Heat the olive oil in a large skillet. Season the outside of the lamb with salt and pepper and sear it in the skillet, along with the remaining herbs and garlic. Transfer to a roasting pan fitted with a v-rack and roast for about 1 hour. Remove the lamb from the oven and dilute the pan juices with a ladleful of water. Strain the juices and set aside.
Lower the oven temperature to 200°F (100°C), and continue to roast, about 3 hours more. Let the lamb rest before slicing, and serve with the reserved pan juices.

SALADS & VEGETABLES

THE VEGETABLE GARDEN ON YOUR PLATE

There is no other gastronomy in the world that holds vegetables so dearly as Italian cuisine. It is a sincere love, with its roots going back into the mists of time, owing to the precious heritage of agricultural cultivation that the Bel Paese can boast from north to south: from the red radicchio di Treviso to Pachino cherry tomatoes, from the green asparagus of Romagna to Roman artichokes, from Tropea onions to the eggplants of Sicily. And the love for this green wealth has been further reinforced in recent years, because many people have become interested in a vegetarian diet, whether for reasons related to health, ethics, or the environment. Not only has the Bel Paese's gastronomic culture always made use of produce from the garden to prepare the various dishes that make up a meal, but it has even succeeded in making them the stars of side dishes. Here, they are enjoyed raw or cooked by various methods, whether steamed, stewed, sautéed, baked au gratin, marinated, fried, sautéed "truffle-style," or grilled, and served on their own or combined with other ingredients. As a side dish, vegetables accompany a main course dish of meat or fish, but may also be considered lighter, flavorsome main courses in and of themselves. This is particularly so if they are reinforced by protein ingredients, like baked potatoes filled with fresh goat cheese, or or fennel au gratin, flavored with butter and a generous sprinkling of Parmigiano-Reggiano. Naturally, if a side dish is served as a side, it should be presented in a reduced quantity, so as to maintain a certain harmony of proportions with the main dish it accompanies. If instead, it is to assume the dignity of a main course, the quantity can be increased. These vegetable-based recipes, so typically Italian, are not only a fantasy of colors, textures, and fragrances, but a treasure trove of taste, and should be prepared using seasonal ingredients. They should also be correctly matched with the dishes they are to accompany, selected for their affinity or contrast, but never for homogeneity, so as to "escort" the main dish, to its side or in front of it.

1 3/4 lbs. (800 g)
  asparagus
1/2 stick (60 g) unsalted
  butter
2 oz. (50 g) grated
  Parmigiano-Reggiano,
  or about 1/2 cup
salt

Difficulty: 1

Preparation: 15 minutes
Cooking: 10 minutes

PARMA STYLE ASPARAGUS

Bring a pot of well-salted water to a boil.
Trim the hard ends from the asparagus and cut all of the stalks the same length.
Tie the asparagus in small bundles with butcher's twine and boil, with the tips pointing upward to avoid damage, until tender but still firm, about 10 minutes.
Drain, remove the twine, and arrange the asparagus on a serving dish.
Sprinkle the asparagus tips with the Parmigiano-Reggiano.
In a small saucepan, melt the butter and cook until frothy. Pour it over the asparagus and serve.

1 lb. (500 g) **eggplant**, diced
7 oz. (200 g) **red onion**, diced
14 oz. (400 g) **red bell peppers**, diced
10 1/2 oz. (300 g) **ripe tomatoes**, diced
3 1/2 oz. (100 g) **black olives**
3 1/2 oz. (100 g) **raisins**, or about 2/3 cup packed
1 oz. (30 g) **pine nuts**, or about 3 1/2 tbsp., toasted
1 **bunch fennel**, diced
1/3 cup (80 ml) **red wine vinegar**
1/3 cup (80 ml) **extra-virgin olive oil**
2 cloves **garlic**
1/2 oz. (15 g) **fresh basil**, or about 30 leaves
salt and pepper

Difficulty: 1

Preparation: 30 minutes
Cooking: 20 minutes

EGGPLANT SALAD WITH FENNEL, OLIVES, AND RAISINS

Clean and dice each vegetable separately. In a small bowl of warm water, soak the raisins for 15 minutes; then drain them and squeeze out any excess liquid.

Heat the oil in a pan over medium heat and sauté the onion. Add the eggplant, peppers, fennel and garlic and let cook until the eggplant softens, about 10 minutes. Add the olives and raisins, and then add the tomatoes. Stir in the basil, and season salt and pepper.

Cover the pan and let the liquid reduce for 5 minutes, stirring occasionally. Remove the cover, add the sugar and vinegar, and let the vegetables continue to cook until the mixture is dense and the vegetables are tender. Garnish with basil and pine nuts and serve.

JEWISH STYLE ARTICHOKES

Difficulty: 1

Preparation: 20 minutes
Cooking: 25 minutes

4 SERVINGS

1 1/2 lbs. (600 g) **globe artichokes**
3 1/2 oz. (100 g) **lemon**, juiced
extra-virgin olive oil, as needed
salt and pepper

Remove the hard outer leaves of the artichokes, and trim the stem, leaving about 1 inch (3 cm).

With a very sharp knife, trim all around the head of each artichoke to remove the hard part of the leaves. In a bowl, combine the lemon juice with water and put the cut artichokes in the water so they don't turn brown.

Clip a deep fat/candy thermometer to the side of a large skillet. Add enough of the oil so the artichokes will be immersed when added to the pan. Heat the oil to about 270°F (130°C).

Drain and dry the artichokes. Knock them against each other and then flatten them lightly on a chopping board by pressing on the base so the leaves spread out. Sprinkle a pinch of salt and pepper inside the leaves that are no longer tightly closed.

Fry the artichokes in the oil until you can easily insert a knife in the flesh, about 20 minutes. Transfer to paper towels to drain. Just before serving, heat the oil to 340°-350°F (170-180°C) and fry the artichokes again until crunchy, 3-5 minutes. Drain on paper towels and serve hot.

3 1/3 lbs (1.5 kg) **broccoli rabe**, trimmed and chopped into large pieces

10 tsp. (50 ml) **extra-virgin olive oil**

2 cloves **garlic**, thinly sliced

chili peppers to taste

salt

Difficulty: 1

Preparation: 15 minutes

Cooking: 10 minutes

STIR-FRIED BROCCOLI RABE

Heat the extra-virgin olive oil in a skillet with the finely sliced garlic and the chili pepper, and cook until the garlic is golden; do not let the garlic brown too much. Add the broccoli rabe, season with salt, and cook over medium heat, stirring frequently, 10 minutes. Serve.

14 oz. (400 g) **fennel bulbs**
3.5 oz. (100 g) **Parmigiano-Reggiano**, grated, or about 1 cup
3 1/2 tbsp. (50 g) **unsalted butter**
salt

BAKED FENNEL WITH PARMIGIANO-REGGIANO

Difficulty: 1

Preparation: 10 minutes
Cooking: 20 minutes

Heat the oven to 375°F (190°C).
Bring a pot of well-salted water to a boil. Cook the fennel in the boiling water until crisp-tender, then drain. Let cool and cut into thick slices.
Grease a baking dish with some of the butter, then melt the remaining butter in a small saucepan. In the baking dish, arrange a layer of fennel. Sprinkle with part of the grated Parmigiano-Reggiano and a bit of the melted butter. Add a second layer of fennel and continue in the same manner until you have used all of the ingredients.
Bake the fenel until browned, crust, for about 10 minutes. Serve immediately.

1 lb. (500 g) **porcini mushrooms**
5 tsp. (25 ml) **extra-virgin olive oil**
1 clove **garlic**
1 tbsp. **fresh parsley**, chopped
salt and pepper

Difficulty: 1

Preparation: 20 minutes
Cooking: 5-6 minutes

FRIED MUSHROOMS WITH GARLIC AND PARSLEY

Trim the mushrooms and clean them thoroughly, removing the soil and wiping them with a damp cloth. Slice them about 1/12 inch (2mm) thick.
Heat the olive oil in a skillet and sauté the chopped garlic until fragrant; do not burn it. Add the mushrooms and the parsley and cook until the mushrooms are tender. Season to taste with salt and pepper and serve.

POTATO SALAD

Peel the potatoes, cut them into 1-inch cubes, and put them in a serving bowl. In another bowl, mix the yogurt with the extra-virgin olive oil and a pinch of salt. Dress the potatoes with the sauce. Arrange the salad on a serving plate, decorating it with strands of fresh chives, and serve.

1 1/3 lbs. (600 g) **yellow, white, and purple potatoes**, boiled with the skins on
1/3 cup plus 1 1/2 tbsp. (100 ml) **plain yogurt**
1/3 cup plus 1 1/2 tbsp. (100 ml) **extra-virgin olive oil**
Fresh chives, for garnish
salt

Difficulty: 1

Preparation: 20 minutes

VEGETARIAN STACKS

Difficulty: 1

Preparation: 30 minutes
Cooking: 15 minutes

10 oz. (300 g) **ripe tomatoes**
7 oz. (200 g) **yellow bell peppers**
5 oz. (150 g) **grated celeriac**
7 oz. (200 g) **summer squash**
5 oz. (150 g) **radicchio**
7 oz. (200 g) **fennel**
9 oz. (250 g) **zucchini**
6 small **eggplants**

7 oz. (200 g) **red onions**
7 oz. (200 g) **leeks**, white parts only
generous 1/3 cup (100 ml) **milk**
3 tbsp. (50 ml) **extra-virgin olive oil**
All-purpose flour
Vegetable oil for frying
salt and pepper

Cut the white parts of the leeks into thin strips. Soak for 10 minutes in the milk, then drain. Coat in flour. Bring a skillet of oil to a boil and deep-fry the leeks. Drain on a paper towel, season with salt, and set aside. Roast or grill the peppers, peppers in the oven or grill them, then peel them and slice them into rounds. Slice the eggplant, onion, and zucchini into rounds of about 1/8-inch (3 mm) thick. Slice the celeriac and squash, then, using a pastry cutter, slice them into discs the same size as the other vegetables. Slice the tomatoes, fennel, and radicchio.
Put a few drops of water into a pot of salted boiling water, and cook the celeriac for 5 minutes. In another pan of boiling water, parboil the pumpkin for one minute. Heat the oven to 475°F (245°C). Drizzle the eggplant, onion, zucchini, celeriac, squash, fennel, and radicchio with olive oil and roast in a roasting pan for about 35 minutes. (Grilling the vegetables is an option). Place all the cooked vegetables in a bowl, season with salt and pepper and a drizzle of oil and let marinate for at least 15 minutes. Layer vegetables to create stacks. Garnish with the deep-fried leeks and serve.

7 oz. (200 g) **arugula**
5 oz. (150 g) **Parmigiano-Reggiano**
3 1/2 tbsp. (50 ml) **extra-virgin olive oil**
1 tbsp. (15 ml) **balsamic vinegar**
salt and pepper

Difficulty: 1

Preparation: 15 minutes

ARUGULA SALAD WITH PARMIGIANO-REGGIANO

In a small bowl, whisk together the balsamic vinegar, salt, pepper, and oil.
Thinly shave the Parmigiano-Reggiano with a vegetable peeler.
Arrange the arugula on individual plates and sprinkle with the cheese. Drizzle with the dressing and serve.

1 3/4 lbs. (800 g) **potatoes**
5 oz. (150 g) **fresh goat cheese**
salt and pepper

POTATOES STUFFED WITH GOAT CHEESE

Heat the oven to 350°F(180°C). Wrap them potatoes individually, skin on, in aluminum foil. and bake for about 30 minutes. When cool enough to handle, cut them open. Season with a pinch of salt, top each with some of the fresh goat cheese and a sprinkle of pepper, and serve.

Difficulty: 1

Preparation: 10 minutes
Cooking: 30 minutes

DESSERTS

A FINALE... IN SWEETNESS

Little delights of pastry crust, held together by an elegant veil of chocolate. Delicate and voluptuous waves of cream you could dive into. Inviting geometric forms of sweetness to could get lost in. Cakes with crispy centers of dried fruits and treasure chests of puff pastry with unexpectedly fragrant fillings. Refreshing and colorful scoops of ice cream and soft sorbet. Fruit scrumptiously covered with chocolate, or lavishly filled with sweetness.

Just think how much creativity would be gone from cooking if we did not have desserts. The Italian cuisine, in particular, would be bereft of large part of its glorious tradition.

All of the regions of the Bel Paese, in fact, have the good fortune of a rich legacy of traditional sweets, from the simplest, most ordinary, and easy to make to the most elaborate, spectacular, and time-consuming: the small pastry and many fried delights and spoon desserts, the bewitching cakes, the classic donuts, and the rustic tarts. Then there are the ever-so-Italian family of ice creams, sorbets, and soft ice creams, and the lighter preparations made from fresh fruits.

There are also the "specialty" desserts, usually only available locally in limited areas, which nearly always emerged as ritual symbols linked with sacred events. At one time limited to religious festivals or private events, these now can be commonly found in pastry shops and private homes in their territory of origin. Other recipes, while representing local or regional pride, are so well known and widespread along the peninsula that they have become national delicacies. There is Apple Strudel, representing Alto Adige; the delicious Cannoli, a veritable masterpiece of Sicilian pastry making; the Baci di Dama cookies with cacao and Zabaglione, Piedmontese delicacies; the Sbrisolona cake, a star dessert from Mantua; the Cantucci with almonds, traditionally to be dipped in Vin Santo, the glory of Prato and Tuscany; and the delectable Tiramisu, with its origins in the Veneto region.

Dessert is becoming increasingly important in the Italian meal. Not as a necessity, but it certainly is pleasant. Perhaps also for its almost therapeutic nature, and not simply for its gourmet attraction. A dessert doesn't merely delight the palate; it warms and cuddles the soul.

LADY'S KISSES

Difficulty: 2

Preparation: 40 minutes
Resting: 30 minutes
Cooking: 15 minutes

4 Servings

1 cup (125 g) **all-purpose flour**
1/2 cup plus 2 tbsp. (125 g) **sugar**
3/4 cup (100 g) **roasted hazelnuts**
scant 1/4 cup (25 g) **blanched almonds**
generous 1/2 cup (125 g) **unsalted butter**, softened
1/4 cup plus 2 tbsp. (30 g) **cocoa powder**
3 1/2 oz. (100 g) **dark chocolate**, roughly chopped

In a blender, pulse the hazelnuts and almonds with the sugar until finely ground. Transfer the mixture to a bowl and mix with the butter.
Sift the flour and cocoa powder together, then incorporate into the nut mixture, stirring as little as possible. Wrap the mixture in plastic wrap and refrigerate for at least 30 minutes.
Heat the oven to 325°F (160°C).
Using a rolling pin, roll out the mixture on a lightly floured pastry board to a thickness of about 3/8 inch (1 cm). Cut out discs with pastry rings 5/8 to 3/4 inch (1.5 to 2 cm) in diameter and shape into balls with your hands.
Butter and flour a baking sheet or line it with parchment paper. Arrange the balls on the baking sheet and bake for about 15 minutes. Let cool completely, then remove the balls from the pan and turn them upside-down.
Meanwhile, melt the chocolate in a heatproof bowl that fits snugly over a pot of barely simmering water (or in the microwave). Let the chocolate cool and when it starts to thicken, pour a little on each of half of baci di dama. Gently press the remaining baci di dama on top of the chocolate and let set.

CREAM PUFFS

Preparation: 25 minutes
Cooking: 20 minutes

4 Servings

FOR THE PUFFS
generous 1/4 cup plus 2 tbsp. (100 ml)
water
3 1/2 tbsp. (50 g) **unsalted butter**, cut
into pieces
1/2 cup (60 g) **all-purpose flour**
2 large **eggs**
salt

FOR THE CREAM FILLING
4 cups (500 ml) **milk**
3/4 cup (150 g) **sugar**
4 large **egg yolks**
generous 1/8 cup (20 g) **all-purpose
flour**, sifted
2 1/2 tbsp. (20 g) **cornstarch**, sifted
1/2 **vanilla bean**, split

Bring the water to a boil in a pan with the butter and a pinch of salt. Sift the flour, and when the water is boiling, add it all at once, then stir with a whisk. When the mixture begins to thicken, switch to a wooden spoon and continue to cook over medium heat until the mixture no longer sticks to the sides of the pan, 2 to 3 minutes. Remove from the heat, let cool slightly, then stir in the eggs one at a time, only adding the second egg when the first one has been completely incorporated.

Heat the oven to 375°F (190°C) and butter a baking sheet. Fill a pastry bag fitted with a 1/4 in (6-7 mm) smooth tip. Pipe the cream puff mixture onto the baking sheet and bake for about 20 minutes.

Meanwhile, prepare the filling. Bring the milk to the boil in a pan with the vanilla bean. In a bowl, beat the egg yolks with the sugar with a whisk.

Incorporate the cornstarch and flour. Pour about a quarter of the boiling milk mixture into the egg yolk mixture and stir until the mixture is perfectly combined. Then pour this mixture into the rest of the milk and return to the heat. Return to a boil and continue to cook, whisking constantly. Pour the cooked cream filling into a bowl and let it cool it quickly.

To assemble the cream puffs, put the filling in a pastry bag fitted with a tip. Cut the top off each cream puff and fill with the cream. Serve.

SICILIAN CANNOLI

Difficulty: 2

Preparation: 28 minutes

Resting: 30 minutes

Cooking: 2 minutes

4 Servings

FOR THE DOUGH
3/4 cup plus 1 tbsp. (100 g) **pastry flour**
2 tbsp. (10 g) **unsweetened cocoa**
3 1/2 tsp. (15 g) **sugar**
1 large **egg**
1 tbsp. **marsala wine** or rum
1 tbsp. (10 g) **unsalted butter**
1 pinch **salt**

FOR THE FILLING
9 oz. (250 g) **fresh ricotta** (preferably made from sheep's milk)
1/2 cup (100 g) **sugar**
1 oz. (25 g) candied fruit, **roughly** chopped
1 oz. (25 g) **dark chocolate**, roughly chopped
1 oz. (25 g) **pistachio nuts**, roughly chopped
olive oil for frying, as needed
confectioners' sugar, for decorating

Combine the flour, cocoa, butter, egg, sugar, and a pinch of salt on a work surface; then add the marsala and continue to knead. When the dough is homogeneous, let it rest for about 30 minutes.

Meanwhile, prepare the filling: Pass the ricotta through a sieve into a bowl, stir in the other filling ingredients, and refrigerate.

Roll out the dough and cut it into 4-inch (10 cm) squares. Wrap the squares diagonally around metal cannoli tubes.

Pour enough oil into a Dutch oven or other heavy pot so that it will be deep enough to submerge the cannoli. Heat the oil, and when hot, fry the cannoli for 1-2 minutes. As soon as the dough becomes golden, remove from the oil, drain on paper towels, and let cool. Then remove them from the metal tubes.

Spoon the cannoli filling into a pastry bag and fill the cannoli. Dust with confectioners' sugar and serve immediately. (After some time, the humidity of the filling will make the dough lose its crispness.)

VANILLA AND CHOCOLATE ICE CREAM

Preparation: 20 minutes

Maturation: 6 hours

INGREDIENTS FOR APPROXIMATELY 2 PINTS (900 ML) OF ICE CREAM

FOR THE CHOCOLATE

2 1/8 cups (500 ml) **milk**
2/3 cup (130 g) **sugar**
2 oz. (50 g) **unsweetened cocoa**, or about 1/2 cup

1/2 oz. (15 g) **dextrose**, or about 6 tsp.
1/8 oz. (3.5 g) **stabilizer**, or about 1 tsp.
1/3 oz. (10 g) **dark chocolate**, chopped

Prepare an ice bath by filling a large bowl with several inches of ice water. Set a smaller metal bowl in the ice water.
Heat the milk to 115°F (45°C); check with an instant read thermometer. In a bowl, combine the sugar, dextrose, and stabilizer, and pour the mixture into the milk in a steady stream. Heat the milk mixture to 150°F (65°C) and continue to cook until it reaches 185°F (85°C). Stir in the chocolate. Transfer the mixture to the bowl in the ice bath and cool rapidly. Refrigerate at 40°F (4°C) for six hours and then freeze the mixture in an ice cream maker according to the manufacturer's instructions.

FOR THE VANILLA

2 cups plus 2 tbsp. (500 ml) **milk**
3 large **egg yolks**
3/4 cup (150 g) **sugar**
1/2 oz. (20 g) **dextrose**, or about 8 tsp.

2 cups plus 2 tsp. (15 g) **powdered skim milk**
1/8 oz. (3.5 g) **stabilizer**, or about 1 tsp.
5 tbsp. (50 g) **heavy cream**
1 **vanilla bean**, split

Heat the milk with the cracked vanilla bean to 115° F (45°C); check with an instant read thermometer and then remove the vanilla bean. Mix the sugar, powdered milk, dextrose and stabilizer and pour the dry mixture in a steady stream into the milk. Heat to 150°F (65°C), add the cream, and continue to cook until it reaches 185°F (85°C). Cool rapidly by putting the mixture in a container and immersing it in an ice water bath. Refrigerate at 40°F (4°C) for six hours and then freeze the mixture in an ice cream maker according to the manufacturer's instructions.

2 cups (250 g) **all-purpose flour**
3/4 cup plus 2 tbsp. (175 g) **sugar**
4 1/2 oz. (125 g) **almonds**
1/2 tsp. (2 g) **baking soda**
2 (95 g) large **eggs**
2 (30 g) large **egg yolks**
1 pinch (1 g) **salt**
pure vanilla extract, to taste

Difficulty: 2

Preparation: 20 minutes
Cooking: 20 minutes

ALMOND COOKIES

Heat the oven to 350°F (180°C) Line a baking sheet with parchment.
Mix all the ingredients together and knead them together until the dough is smooth and homogeneous. Form the dough into logs and arrange them on the baking sheet. Bake for about 20 minutes. While the logs are still hot, cut them into into diagonal slices. Return them to the oven and bake until golden on both sides.

BAKED APPLES WITH RAISINS AND ALMONDS

1 1/2 lbs. (700 g) **apples,** such as Reinette or Golden Delicious
3 oz. (80 g) **apricot preserves,** or about 1/4 cup
1 1/2 oz. (40 g) **raisins,** or about 1/4 cup packed
1 1/2 oz. (40 g) **slivered almonds,** or about 1/3 cup
2 tbsp. (25 g) **brown sugar**

Difficulty: 1

Preparation: 20 minutes
Cooking: 30 minutes

Heat the oven to 325°F (160°C).
Make a circular incision around each apple with the tip of a knife so it doesn't burst in the oven. Remove the core with an apple corer.
In a bowl, stir together the raisins and preserves and fill each apple with the mixture. Sprinkle the brown sugar on top.
Arrange the apples in a baking dish, sprinkle the almonds over the tops, and bake for about 15 minutes.

MILK CHOCOLATE MOUSSE

Difficulty: 2

Preparation: 45 minutes

Cooling: 3 hours

Cooking: 50 minutes

6 SERVINGS

FOR THE MOUSSE
1 cup (250 ml) **milk**
2 large **egg yolks**
9 oz. (250 g) **milk chocolate**, chopped
7 oz. (200 g) **semi-whipped cream**
1/3 oz. (10 g) **gelatin sheets**

FOR THE BATTER
1/2 cup (100 g) **sugar**
3 large **eggs**

1 large **egg yolk**
2/3 cup (80 g) **all-purpose flour**
2 1/2 tbsp. (20 g) **potato starch** or
cornstarch
3 tbsp. (15 g) **unsweetened cocoa powder**

FOR THE SYRUP
2 tbsp. (30 ml) **water**
3/8 cup (80 g) **sugar**
2 1/2 tbsp. (35 ml) **rum** (or other liqueur)

Heat the oven to 450°F (230°C). Line a baking sheet with parchment.
To make the dough for the chocolate layer, sift together the flour, starch, and cocoa. Separate the eggs and whisk the egg whites in a bowl with the sugar. In another bowl, stir the egg yolks with a fork. Fold in the egg whites, then add the flour mixture. Transfer to the baking sheet and spread so that the mixture is about 3/8 inch (1 cm) thick. Bake for 5 to 7 minutes.
To make the syrup, bring the water and sugar to a boil in a saucepan. Boil until the sugar is dissolved and remove from the heat. When cooled, stir in the rum and set aside.
To make the mousse, put the chopped chocolate in a bowl. Soften the gelatin in a bowl of cold water. Add the egg yolks and the milk and cook over low heat to pasteurize the mixture, stirring constantly, until it reaches 185°F (85°C); check with an instant read thermometer. Remove from heat. Squeeze the gelatin, and add it to the mixture so that it melts. Immediately pour the mixture onto the chopped chocolate and stir thoroughly to obtain a smooth, even texture. Let cool to 86°F (30°C).
Whip the cream, which must stay fairly soft, then gently fold it into the chocolate mixture with a spatula.
To assemble, line the bottom and sides of a springform pan with the dough and drench it with syrup. Fill with mousse, smooth it with a spatula, and refrigerate for at least 3 hours. Remove from the mold and decorate as desired.
Cover the top with chocolate curls if desired.

CHOCOLATE BULL'S-EYES

Difficulty: 2

Preparation: 1 hour
Resting: 1 hour
Cooking: 13-15 minutes

<small>INGREDIENTS FOR **12** COOKIES</small>

FOR THE CHOCOLATE SHORTBREAD
1 1/4 cups (165 g) **all-purpose flour**
1/4 cup plus 2 tbsp. (95 g) **unsalted butter**, softened
generous 1/4 cup plus 2 tbsp. (85 g) **sugar**
2 large **egg yolks**
1/4 tsp. (1 g) **baking powder**
7 tsp. (9 g) **unsweetened cocoa powder**
Pinch **vanilla powder**
salt

FOR THE FILLING
2 tbsp. (30 g) **orange marmalade**

FOR THE GANACHE
2 oz. (60 g) **dark chocolate**, chopped
4 tbsp. (60 ml) **heavy cream**
1 tsp. (6 ml) **glucose syrup**

Sift the flour and baking powder onto a piece of parchment. In a bowl, mix the butter with the sugar, stirring in a pinch of salt and the egg yolks. Add flour sifted with baking powder, the vanilla powder, and cocoa powder, and then knead briefly until you have a smooth dough.
Wrap the dough in plastic wrap and refrigerate for at least 1 hour.
Heat the oven to 350°F (180°C) and grease and flour (or line with parchment) two baking sheets. On a lightly floured work surface, roll out the dough until just under 1/4 inch (4-5 mm) thick. Using a pastry ring with a 2-inch (5 cm) diameter, cut out discs (you'll need two discs for each finished bull's-eye).
Divide the dough discs equally between the baking sheets. Using a pastry ring with a 1 1/2 inch (4 cm) diameter, make a hole in the center of each disc on the first pan so that you have rings. Transfer the pans to the oven and bake for 12 to 13 minutes, removing pan with rings a couple of minutes earlier than the one with discs. Let cool completely.
Turn the discs over and spread them with orange marmalade. Top with the rings (the marmalade will ensure that they adhere).
To make the ganache, put the chocolate in a bowl. In a small saucepan, bring the cream to a boil with the glucose syrup. Pour the hot mixture over the chocolate. Let cool slightly, put the ganache in a pastry bag fitted with a tip, and fill the cavity of the bull's-eyes.

CHOCOLATE-COVERED ALMONDS AND HAZELNUTS

Difficulty: 1

Preparation: 40 minutes

4 Servings

1 1/2 tbsp. (20 g) **sugar**
2 tsp. (10 ml) **water**
1 cup (125 g) **almonds and hazelnuts**
1 tsp. (5 g) **unsalted butter**
6 oz. (180 g) **dark chocolate**, melted

Put the sugar and water in a saucepan and bring to a boil.
Add the almonds and hazelnuts, then cook until the sugar is amber in color. Stir in the butter, then pour the mixture onto a baking sheet to cool, separating the almonds and hazelnuts.
Once the nuts have cooled, put them in a large bowl and add about a quarter of the chocolate.
Stir so that the chocolate does not solidify, keeping the almonds and hazelnuts well separated.
Repeat until you have finished adding all of the chocolate. Transfer the chocolate-coated nuts to a large-mesh sieve set over a bowl, and let the excess chocolate drain off. Transfer the nuts to parchment and let them set. Store in a dry place at room temperature, preferably in sealed glass jars or in cans with a lid.

FOR THE MERINGUE
1/4 cup plus 2 1/2 tbsp.
   (80 g) **sugar**
2 tbsp. plus 2 tsp. (40 g)
   large **egg whites**
1 tbsp. plus 1 tsp. (20 ml)
   water

FOR THE MOUSSE
2/3 cup plus 1 tbsp. (170
   ml) **heavy cream**
1/4 cup plus 2 tsp. (70 ml)
   lemon juice
1/3 oz. (10 g) **gelatin
   sheets**
1 tbsp. plus 1 tsp. (20 ml)
   extra-virgin olive oil

Difficulty: 1

Preparation: 30 minutes

Freezing: 2 hours

LEMON MOUSSE WITH
EXTRA-VIRGIN OLIVE OIL

To make the meringue, add the water and 1/3 cup of the sugar to a small saucepan and bring to a boil. Meanwhile, in a stand mixer or using an electric hand mixer, beat the egg whites with the remaining sugar in a bowl. (Alternatively, you can use a whisk.) When the sugar water reach 250°F (121°C)—check with an instant read thermometer—slowly add it to the egg whites and keep beating until it cools.

Soak the gelatin in cold water for 5 minutes, then slowly dissolve it in a saucepan over low heat or in the microwave. Whip the heavy cream and fold it into the meringue along with the gelatin and lemon juice.

Pour the mixture into individual molds and freeze them until set, about 2 hours. Unmold the mousse onto serving plates and drizzle with extra-virgin olive oil before serving.

PANNA COTTA

4 SERVINGS

1/2 cup (125 ml) **milk**
1/2 cup (125 ml) **heavy cream**
3 1/2 tbsp. (50 g) **sugar**
1 sheet (1/5 oz.) **gelatin**

Difficulty: 1

Preparation: 20 minutes
Resting: 3 hours

In a saucepan, bring the milk, cream and sugar to a boil.
Meanwhile, soak the gelatin in a bowl of cold water. Squeeze it out, and add the gelatin to the milk mixture. Stir well, taking care to avoid froth forming, and then pour the mixture into individual molds. Refrigerate for several hours.
Unmold the panna cotta and serve. Try garnishing with a chocolate or caramel sauce, or with a fruit sauce made with strawberries, kiwis, or pears. Alternatively, sprinkle with chopped hazelnuts or pistachios.

1 lb. (500 g) **peaches**
5 **amaretti cookies**,
  crushed
3 tbsp. plus 2 tsp. (20 g)
  unsweetened cocoa
2 large **eggs**
1/4 cup plus 1 1/2 tbsp. (70
  g) **sugar**

Difficulty: 1

Preparation: 20 minutes
Cooking: 30 minutes

PEACHES STUFFED
WITH AMARETTI COOKIES

Heat the oven to 325°F (160°C) and line a baking sheet with parchment.
Halve the peaches, remove the pits, and use a spoon to scoop out a bit more flesh from the center. Chop it up and mix it with the 2 egg yolks, amaretti and cocoa.
In a bowl with an electric mixer, beat the egg whites with the sugar until stiff peaks form. Fold them into the amaretti mixture.
Arrange the peach halves on the prepared baking sheet. Fill with the amaretti mixture and bake for about 30 minutes. Serve warm or cold.

FOR THE PEELS
4 1/2 oz. (130 g) **candied orange peel**, quartered

FOR THE GLAZE
2 1/2 oz. (70 g) **dark chocolate**

CHOCOLATE-COVERED ORANGE PEELS

Arrange the candied orange peel quarters on a wire rack and let dry at room temperature overnight. The next day, cut them into strips about 1/4 inch (5-6 mm) wide and temper the dark chocolate: Melt the chocolate in a bain marie or microwave at 113-122°F (45-50°C) (use a cooking thermometer). Pour one-third to one-half onto a marble surface. Let this cool until it reaches 79-81°F (26-27°C), then add it on top of the remaining hot chocolate. When the temperature of this new mixture reaches 86-88°F (30-31°C), it is ready to be used. Glaze the candied orange peels in the tempered chocolate using a fork. Drain the excess chocolate and place the chocolate-covered orange peels on a sheet of parchment. Let set at room temperature.

Difficulty: 1

Preparation: 12 hours

1 1/4 cups (300 g) **confectioners' cream** (see recipe below)

7 cups (415 g) **unsweetened whipped cream**

About 1/2 cup (135 g) **Italian style meringue** (see recipe below)

3 oz. (80 g) **hazelnut paste**

FOR THE CREAM
2 large **egg yolks**
6 tbsp. (75 g) **sugar**
2 tbsp. (28 g) **all-purpose flour**
1 cup (250 ml) **milk**

FOR THE MERINGUE
2 large **egg whites**
1/2 cup plus 1 tbsp. (120 g) **sugar**
4 tsp. (20 ml) **water**

Difficulty: 3

Preparation: 1 hour
Freezing: 3 hours

PIEDMONT HAZELNUT SEMIFREDDO

To prepare the Italian style meringue, clip a thermometer to the side of a small saucepan and heat two-thirds of the sugar and the water. Meanwhile, whisk the egg whites in a bowl with the remaining sugar until stiff. When the sugar mixture in the saucepan reaches 250°F (120°C)— check with an instant read thermometer—pour it onto the whipped egg whites and continue to whisk until lukewarm. Set aside.

To make the confectioner's cream, beat the egg yolks in a bowl with the sugar, add the flour, and mix. In a small saucepan, bring the milk to a boil. Add a little milk to the beaten yolks and mix until the yolks are warm; add back to the rest of the hot milk and mix thoroughly. Cool the mixture rapidly. Stir in the hazelnut paste. Carefully blend the mixture with the Italian meringue, and then gently stir in the unsweetened whipped cream. Pour the mixture into individual molds and freeze for at least three hours. Unmold and serve.

4 SERVINGS

9 oz. (250 g) **strawberries**, hulled
1 cup (250 ml) **water**
3/4 cup plus 3 tbsp. (185 g) **sugar**
1/4 **lemon**, quartered

STRAWBERRY SORBET

Squeeze the juice from 1 quarter of the lemon.
Combine the strawberries with the water and sugar in a blender and puree. Add the lemon juice. Refrigerate the mixture for at least 3 hours. Freeze in an ice cream maker according to the manufacturer's instructions.

Difficulty: 1

Preparation: 20 minutes

Freezing: 3 hours

APPLE STRUDEL

4 SERVINGS

FOR THE DOUGH
2 cups (250 g) **all-purpose flour**
2/3 cup (150 ml) **water**
4 tbsp. (20 ml) **extra-virgin olive oil**
Pinch **salt**

FOR THE FILLING
1 3/4 lbs. (800 g) **apples**
3 1/2 oz. (100 g) **raisins**
3 1/2 oz. (100 g) **pine nuts**, or about
2/3 cup

1/2 stick (57 g) **unsalted butter**
2-3 1/2 oz. (57-100 g) **breadcrumbs**, or
1/2-1 cup
cinnamon, as needed

FOR DECORATING
1 large **egg**
confectioners' sugar, as needed

Mix the flour with the water, oil and salt on a work surface and knead until the dough is smooth and homogeneous. Form it into a ball, cover with plastic wrap, and let rest for at least 30 minutes.

Meanwhile, prepare the filling for the strudel. Peel and slice the apples. Soak the raisins in a bowl of lukewarm water for 15 minutes; then drain the raisins and press to remove excess water.

Melt the butter In a large skillet. Add the apple slices, raisins, pine nuts, and a pinch cinnamon. Stir in enough breadcrumbs to reach your desired filling consistency.

Heat the oven to 350°F (180°C) and line a baking sheet with parchment. With the back of your hands, stretch the dough into a thin sheet on a lightly floured work surface. Spoon the filling along the long side of the pastry, leaving a 2 inches (few cm) border and roll it up, making sure it is well sealed by pressing down along the edges with your fingers and curling up the two ends.

In a small bowl, lightly beat the egg with a fork. Brush the strudel with the egg. Set it on the prepared baking sheet and bake for about 20 minutes. A few minutes before it is done, dust with powdered sugar and finish baking. Serve with whipped cream, if you like.

VIENNESE CAKE

Difficulty: 3

Preparation: 45 minutes

Cooking: 45 minutes

4-6 SERVINGS

FOR THE CAKE
3/4 cup (115 g) peeled, **sweet almonds**
1/10 oz (3 g) **bitter almonds** or apricot kernels
generous 2/3 cup (137 g) **sugar**
1/4 cup plus 2 tbsp. (45 g) **all-purpose flour**
1 1/2 tbsp. (12 g) **potato starch** or cornstarch
1/4 cup (25 g) **unsweetened cocoa powder**
vanilla powder
salt
3 oz. (82 g) **dark chocolate**

5 tsp. (25 g) **unsalted butter**
5 large **egg yolks**
4 large **egg whites**

FOR THE FILLING
4 oz. (120 g) **apricot jam**
4 tsp. (20 ml) **orange liqueur**

FOR THE GLAZE
2/3 cup (170 ml) **cream**
5 tsp. (25 ml) **glucose syrup**
6 oz. (170 g) **dark chocolate**

Heat the oven to 350°F (180°C) and grease and flour a 9x5 inch (23x13 cm) pan. In a food processor, finely grind the almonds with 2 tbsp (25 g) of sugar. Transfer to a bowl and then mix in the flour, starch, cocoa, vanilla, and a pinch of salt. Melt the chocolate and butter together in a heatproof bowl that fits snugly over a pot of barely simmering water (or in the microwave). Stir occasionally until the chocolate is melted and smooth; remove from the heat. In a bowl, beat the yolks with 4 tbsp. (50 g) of the sugar. In another bowl, beat the egg whites with 1/3 cup (62 g) of the sugar. Lighten the beaten yolks with one-third of the beaten egg whites, then add the melted chocolate and butter. Combine the mixture with the almonds, flour, starch, and cocoa. Fold in the remaining egg whites. Gently mix, using a soft spatula and stirring from the bottom up. Pour the mixture into a greased, floured pan. Bake for 40 to 45 minutes. Let cool completely. Remove the cake from the pan and cut the cake horizontally into three layers. Make the filling by stirring together the apricot jam and the orange liqueur in a bowl. Spread the filling between the cake layers, and spread more jam over the surface of the cake. To make the glaze, chop the chocolate and put in a heatproof bowl. In a small saucepan, boil the cream with the glucose syrup and then pour over on the chocolate. Stir with a wooden spoon until the mixture is smooth and velvety. Frost the cake with the glaze.

TIRAMISÙ

Difficulty: 2

Preparation: 30 minutes

Resting: 2 hours

4 Servings

4 large **pasteurized egg yolks**
2 large **pasteurized egg whites**
10 tbsp. (125 g) **sugar**
1 cup (250 g) **mascarpone**
5 tsp. (25 ml) **brandy** (optional)
1 cup (200 ml) **sweetened coffee**
8 **savoiardi** (lady fingers)
unsweetened cocoa powder, as needed

In a bowl, beat the eggs yolks with most of the sugar, heating the mixture slightly in a heatproof bowl that fits snugly over a pot of barely simmering water. In another bowl, whisk the egg whites with the remaining sugar.

Stir the mascarpone into the egg yolks, then add the stiff egg whites and carefully fold so the mixture remains light and frothy.

Dip the lady fingers in the sweetened coffee (if you wish you can add a little brandy) and place them in the bottom of a dish (or in four small dishes or glasses). Then pour in a layer of the cream mixture and continue alternating layers of biscuits and cream. Refrigerate the tiramisù for about two hours.

Garnish with a generous sprinkling of cocoa.

3/4 cup plus 1 tbsp. (100 g) **all-purpose flour**

1/4 cup (25 g) finely ground **cornmeal flour**

6 tbsp. (75 g) **sugar**

2/3 stick (75 g) **unsalted butter**, softened

2 1/2 oz.(75 g) **ground almonds**

1 large **egg yolk**

1 pinch (0.5 g) **baking powder**

14 oz. (25 g) **whole almonds**

grated **lemon zest**, to taste

Difficulty: 1

Preparation: 20 minutes

Cooking: 10 minutes

CRUMBLE CAKE

In a bowl, mix all the ingredients together, except for the whole almonds. Knead to make a crumbly mixture. Put the mixture in a 7 1/2-9 1/2-inch (20-25 cm) diameter mold, pressing down lightly, and decorate with the whole almonds.
Bake in the oven at 350°F (180°C) until the crumble cake is golden, about 18 minutes.

4 large **egg yolks**
2 tbsp. (25 g) **sugar**
generous 3/4 cup (200
    ml) **Moscato d'Asti** or
    other Muscat wine
3/4 cup plus 2 tbsp. (220
    ml) **heavy cream**
2 sheets (1/7 oz.) **gelatin**

Difficulty: 1

Preparation: 15 minutes
Resting: 2 hours
Cooking: 10 minutes

COLD ZABAGLIONE WITH MUSCAT WINE

In a pan, preferably copper, beat the egg yolks lightly with the sugar and wine.
Set the pan over low heat and continue cooking until the zabaglione becomes frothy and has thickened.
Meanwhile, soak the gelatin in cold water, then squeeze out the excess water. Add the gelatin to the egg and wine mixture.
Remove the zabaglione from the heat and let cool. Whip the cream and carefully fold it into the cooled zabaglione. Pour into individual bowls and refrigerate for at least 2 hours before serving.

ALPHABETIC INDEX OF RECIPES

INGREDIENTS INDEX

INGREDIENTS INDEX

Original edition © 2013 by De Agostini S.p.A.

The Taunton Press
Inspiration for hands-on living®

The Taunton Press, Inc.
63 South Main Street
PO Box 5506, Newtown, CT 06470-5506
e-mail: tp@taunton.com

Translations:
Rosetta Translations SARL, John Venerella, Mary Doyle,
Catherine Howard, Salvatore Ciolfi

Editor: Rebecca Freedman

LIBRARY OF CONGRESS CATALOGING-IN-PUBLICATION DATA IN PROGRESS
ISBN: 978-1-62710-086-1

Printed in China
10 9 8 7 6 5 4 3 2 1